'Christobel Mattingley's a fine writer. Yvonne Edwards has the memories of the evil British and Australian bomb testing that changed her family's life forever. This is a very special book to be read by any age group interested in real Australian history.'
— Yami Lester, OAM, nuclear test survivor

'This is a very sad story! It gave me more understanding of the life of my mob during this horrific time in our lives. I felt so much for Yvonne Edwards, her family and her people. But this happened so totally to all our mobs all over our country.'
— Dr Alitya Rigney

'An outstanding work of non-fiction. By recording and documenting the life of a remarkable woman who lived through one of the most deplorable episodes in Australian history, Christobel Mattingley has done the nation a great service... No one who reads this book will forget Yvonne Edwards and her inspirational life. She was a true heroine, of whom all Australians should be proud.'
— Graham Jenkin

'A very moving account of Yvonne Edwards' life story. As the "last man standing" (with difficulty) of the cluster of army chaplains who – like many of Yvonne Edwards' family and friends – died of radiation cancers, I endorse the powerful message of *Maralinga's Long Shadow*. I'm convinced that the Maralinga mistake needs to be made more widely known.'
— The Reverend Canon Peter W Patterson

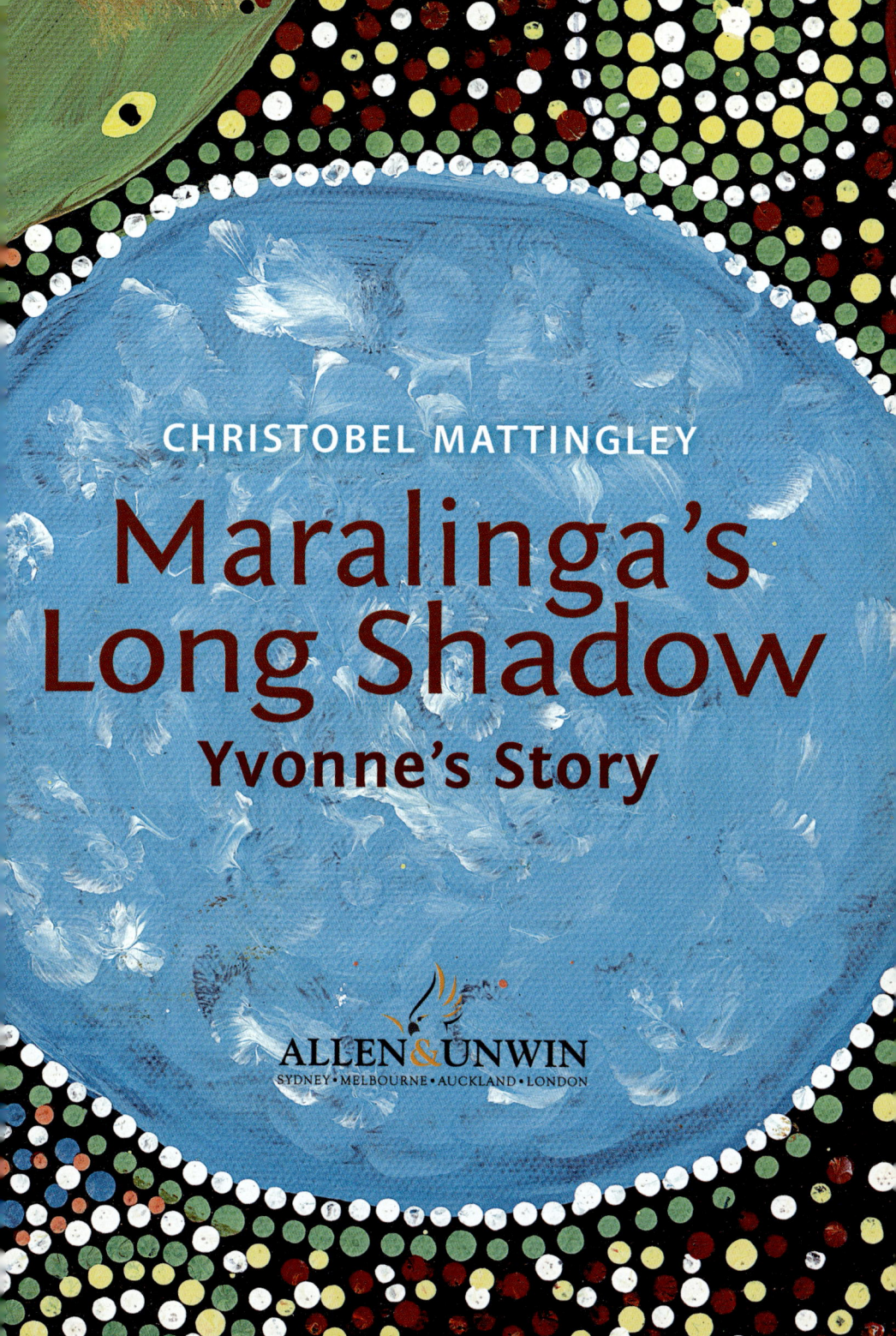

All royalties from the sale of this book have been given to Yvonne Edwards'
five surviving children: Duane, Teddy, Judy, Terence and Aaron Edwards.

First published by Allen & Unwin in 2016

Copyright © Text, Christobel Mattingley 2016

Copyright © All statements and translations, artworks and photographs,
With their authors and creators 2016

Every effort has been made to contact copyright holders. The publisher welcomes
contact with any copyright holders not here acknowledged.

The moral right of Christobel Mattingley to be identified as the author
and of this work has been asserted by her in accordance with the
United Kingdom's *Copyright, Designs and Patents Act 1988*.

All rights reserved. No part of this book may be reproduced or transmitted
in any form or by any means, electronic or mechanical, including photocopying,
recording or by any information storage and retrieval system, without prior permission
in writing from the publisher. The Australian *Copyright Act 1968* (the Act) allows
a maximum of one chapter or ten per cent of this book, whichever is the greater,
to be photocopied by any educational institution for its educational purposes
provided that the educational institution (or body that administers it) has given
a remuneration notice to the Copyright Agency (Australia) under the Act.

Allen & Unwin – Australia
83 Alexander Street, Crows Nest NSW 2065, Australia
Phone: (61 2) 8425 0100
Email: info@allenandunwin.com
Web: www.allenandunwin.com

Allen & Unwin – UK
Ormond House, 26–27 Boswell Street
London WC1N 3JZ, UK

A Cataloguing-in-Publication entry is available from
the National Library of Australia
www.trove.nla.gov.au.

A catalogue record for this book
is available from the British Library

ISBN (AUS) 978 1 76029 017 7
ISBN (UK) 978 1 74336 822 0

Teachers' notes available from www.allenandunwin.com

Cover and text design by Ruth Grüner
Set in 12 pt Caslon 540 by Ruth Grüner
Cover photos: *malukuṟu* by Keturah de Klerk/Photography Life;
mushroom cloud by News Ltd/Newspix

This book was printed in China in December 2015 by Everbest Printing Co., Ltd

1 3 5 7 9 10 8 6 4 2

Supported by Alphaville, assisted by the Australian Government
through the Australia Council, its arts funding and advisory body

Contents

Chapter One
Before Maralinga 1

Chapter Two
A special baby is born 9

Chapter Three
Life at Ooldea 17

Chapter Four
Maralinga 23

Chapter Five
Childhood – good times and bad 29

Chapter Six
Atom bombs on A<u>n</u>angu lands 39

Chapter Seven
Michael 47

Chapter Eight
Marriage and Maralinga 55

Chapter Nine
Refugees, prisoners, and rebuilders of community 69

Chapter Ten
Yvonne the artist 83

Chapter Eleven
Mother to many – caring and sharing 97

Chapter Twelve
The lost is found 115

Chapter Thirteen
The happiest years – Michael 123

Chapter Fourteen
Cancer and the cemetery 129

Chapter Fifteen
Another loss 141

Chapter Sixteen
Maralinga's long shadow 147

Chapter Seventeen
Too young to die 163

Author's note 173
Map 182
Glossary 184
Acknowledgements 186
Sources 188
Timeline 189
Index 195

For Yvonne – with respect,
admiration and love

Chapter One

Before Maralinga

Before Maralinga the A<u>n</u>angu people cared for their country for generation after countless generation. Their land was their being, their spirit, their life. They knew no other. They wanted no other. They loved its rockholes and red sands, its creatures great and small, its trees, its bushes, its flowers, its fruits. Above all they cared for its *kapi*, its water, its precious water, and used it wisely, walking many miles from one rockhole to another, always seeking permission from *Wa<u>n</u>ampi*, the Rainbow Serpent, who guarded each one, before they took the living water.

DETAIL FROM *'WA<u>N</u>AMPI*, THE RAINBOW SERPENT' | ARTWORK BY YVONNE EDWARDS

There were no maps for their journeys. But the Anangu knew their way because they knew the night skies. They knew the stars, which guided them across the sandhills and the scarps. They knew their changing patterns. They knew the signs of the seasons. They knew their changing patterns. From generation to generation they passed on this precious knowledge, sleeping under the stars through all the cycle of the seasons: the burning heat, the biting cold, the devastating droughts, the refreshing but rare rains.

From generation to generation they passed on this precious knowledge, sleeping under the stars through all the cycle of the seasons.

There were no shops, no supermarkets, no money. Anangu had no need of them. They shared all they had. The men hunted game and the women and children gathered seeds, fruit and roots. Men's skilful hands created spears and woomeras (spear-throwers). Women made digging sticks to search out *maku*, the juicy witchetty grubs they loved, as well as yams and bush potatoes. They fashioned *wira* and *piti*, the bowls used for carrying food, water and babies.

ANANGU COUNTRY, NOW AT THE JUNCTION OF MARALINGA AND OAK VALLEY ROADS, SOUTH AUSTRALIA, 2014 | PHOTO BY JESSIE BOYLAN

PAINTINGS OF TRADITIONAL ARTEFACTS (LEFT) AND SITTING DOWN AT WATERHOLES (RIGHT) | ARTWORKS BY YVONNE EDWARDS, PHOTOS BY JESSIE BOYLAN

They celebrated life in songs and stories and dances. And when the waterholes dried up in a searing season of drought, families and travelling groups would gather at the one special place where the water never failed. From the north they would come, from the west and from the east to gather at this special place – *Yuldi* (Ooldea Soak), where the water lay cool and pure beneath the white sand in its beautiful tree-clad valley.

Then *walypala*, whitefellas, came into A<u>n</u>angu lands. *Walypala* who knew nothing about the country. They did not understand it. They called it desert. *Walypala* who knew nothing about its A<u>n</u>angu people, who have one of the oldest living cultures in the world. They had no respect for the Dreamtime Ancestors. They had no knowledge of A<u>n</u>angu *Tjukurpa*, the law which keeps the country and its people strong.

But they had greed. Greed for the land. Greed for the water. They brought their sheep to graze on the feeding grounds of the *ma<u>l</u>u* (red kangaroo), which they hunted with guns for the skins. They took the water for their thirsty sheep. Other *walypala* animals, which had no place on A<u>n</u>angu lands, also came – rabbits, foxes and feral cats. Then when the *walypala* began to build their railway across the A<u>n</u>angu lands, *walypala* came to live at Ooldea and killed the age-old soak with their greed.[*]

> The A<u>n</u>angu celebrated life in songs and stories and dances.

---

[*] In 1912 work commenced on the construction of the Transcontinental Railway from Port Augusta, in what whitefellas called South Australia, to Kalgoorlie, in what they called Western Australia.

And *walypala* men sowed their seed among A*n*angu women.

Other *walypala* also came. Daisy Bates set up her camp near Ooldea, trying to keep A*n*angu from destructive *walypala* assocations, and caring for the frail and sick.* Then missionaries came to tell the A*n*angu that Jesus loved them, and to teach the A*n*angu children *walypala* ways. But as well as Christianity the missionaries brought clothes. Clothes which had to be washed. They also brought rations from the government. Rations which cut across the very fabric of A*n*angu seasonal lifestyle and poisoned the people. Tea, sugar, flour, to which the A*n*angu became addicted, and which kept them sitting down at Ooldea, instead of ranging across their wide hunting grounds, independent of *walypala* and their controlling ways.

BUSH TUCKER WAS ONE OF YVONNE'S FAVOURITE SUBJECTS. TOP, CLOCKWISE FROM TOP LEFT: BLOSSOMS FOR HONEY, *KALTA* (SLEEPY LIZARD), *MAKU* (WITCHETTY GRUBS), *KALAYA* (EMU), *MALU* (RED KANGAROO). BOTTOM, CLOCKWISE FROM TOP LEFT: BLOSSOMS FOR HONEY, *MURUNTU* (SNAKE), *MAKU* (WITCHETTY GRUBS), *MALU* (RED KANGAROO), *KALTA* (SLEEPY LIZARD), *KALAYA* (EMU) | ARTWORKS BY YVONNE EDWARDS, PHOTOS BY JESSIE BOYLAN, COURTESY OF TULLAWON HEALTH SERVICE, YALATA

* Irish-born Daisy Bates began living with an Aboriginal group near Ooldea in 1915. She had already spent many years in Western Australia trying to counteract the effects of whitefella activities on Aboriginal peoples and their lands. In her will, she left royalties from her writing to A*n*angu to help them after her death.

Chapter Two

A special baby is born

In 1950 when the United Aborigines Mission (UAM) had been at Ooldea for 17 years, A*n*angu women who had learned *walypala* ways to cook, clean houses, wear clothes and wash them, still kept their own A*n*angu way of giving birth. So one day when the sun was shining bright in the wide blue sky and the birds were calling in the trees, a group of aunties and grandmothers quietly led a young woman away from the *walypala* buildings and busyness of the mission.

DETAIL FROM '*WA*N*AMPI* FAMILY AT WATERHOLE' | ARTWORK BY YVONNE EDWARDS, PHOTO BY ERICA WAGNER, USED WITH PERMISSION OF DR ALAN & ELIZABETH BRISSENDEN

Slowly they walked, because the young woman they were leading was heavy with child. Her first child. Slowly they walked, bare feet sinking into the soft sand. Slowly they walked, shedding their clothes, singing softly as they went. Back into the bush where mulga and mallee grew thick and green in leafy screen. Back into the bush where the big creamy flowers of the unique Ooldea mallee hummed with bees and wafted their honeyed scent.

They settled in a sheltered spot, surrounding the young woman with their warmth and wisdom, calming her with their crooning, helping her through the pain and pride of giving birth as she squatted on the gentle sand. Hour after slow hour, as shadows grew and their fire gleamed brighter, they encouraged the young mother, stroking her, rubbing her with bush medicine, and singing, always singing.

Then at last it came. The baby they had been waiting to welcome, the cry they had been longing to hear, telling them this child was strong and would grow to be a mother too. Gladly they carried her back to the mission, singing as they went. Gladly she was welcomed by her Anangu family, although she was not as brown as they, and her eyes were not as brown, because her father was a *walypala*.

ABOVE: THE BIG CREAMY FLOWERS OF THE OOLDEA MALLEE | PHOTO BY BILL DOWLING;
OVERLEAF: OAK VALLEY | PHOTO BY TOM STRINGER

But those eyes, sometimes green as mallee leaves, sometimes brown as a wooden *wira*, were the eyes which filled her heart with love for her A̲nangu people, the eyes which filled her mind with the images that one day she would paint. This baby would grow up to grace her people with her courage and passion for justice, and to give *walypala* a way of discovering and beginning to understand her people through her paintings.

> This baby would grow up to grace her people with her courage and passion for justice.

This baby the missionaries named Yvonne. But her A̲nangu family called her Tjintjiwara. According to the calendar of the missionaries she was born on 12 September 1950. But her A̲nangu people measured the passing of time in a different way. In the cycle of the seasons which meant so much to them, this baby was born when *ma̲luku̲ru* carpeted the earth with its flame-like flowers bright against its silver foliage, and all her life Tjintjiwara loved these flowers above any others.*

---

* What *walypala* call Sturt's desert pea, the A̲nangu call *ma̲luku̲ru*, meaning 'kangaroo eyes', because of their shiny, raised black centres.

YVONNE'S FAVOURITE FLOWER, *MALUKURU* (STURT'S DESERT PEA) | PHOTO BY KETURAH DE KLERK/PHOTOGRAPHY LIFE

Chapter Three

Life at Ooldea

Yvonne's first two years were spent in the loving care and nurture of her A̲n̲angu family at Ooldea, listening to their laughter and talk, learning her mother tongue Pitjantjatjara, watching deft hands making damper, skinning rabbits, carving artefacts, drawing in the sand...

She had fondest memories of her strong grandmother, Rene Sandimar, wise in the ways of her people and their Dreamtime Ancestors, warm in her love for her little hazel-eyed granddaughter. At night as they settled around the camp fire, she would hollow out a place in the

DETAIL FROM 'TEACHING *INMA* (DANCE)', 2008, SHOWING ELDER WOMEN TEACHING THE YOUNG GIRLS *INMA*. TOP GROUP WITH OCHRE POT FOR PAINTING DANCERS. BELOW ARE TWO WOMEN HOLDING A *KUTURU* AT EACH END. TWO GIRLS FACE THE STICK AND DANCE. | ARTWORK BY YVONNE EDWARDS, PHOTO BY PAM DIMENT, COURTESY OF TJUTJUNA ARTS & CULTURE CENTRE

sand close beside her for the little girl to sleep, and cover her with her own coat to keep her snug through the chilly darkness. Yvonne carried this precious memory with her throughout her life. 'This old lady used to give me her coat every night. She slept without any covering. She wanted me to sleep warm.' In later life Yvonne herself kept many people warm with her protective love.

Yvonne also began picking up English from the older children in the mission dormitory, listening to their chatter, hearing them sing the hymns the missionaries taught them. *'What a friend we have in Jesus'* echoed in her heart and this loving Jesus did indeed become her lifelong friend.

But without warning, life at Ooldea was brought to an end for its A<u>n</u>angu people. Suddenly they were forcibly removed from this ancient oasis, cut off from its life-giving waters which had sustained their ancestors through countless cruel droughts. All because two groups of *walypala*, people in faraway cities, which A<u>n</u>angu did not even know existed, could not solve their differences. The United Aborigines Mission executive ordered the South Australian branch to close its mission at Ooldea.

LAKE IFOULD, SOUTH-EAST OF MARALINGA | PHOTO BY PAM DIMENT

On 24 June 1952 the A̱nangu were told to leave. It was a turbulent day of deep distress. They wept and wailed, and over 60 years on they still wail at the memory of the betrayal, and how they were forced to leave. East, west, north, south they went or were sent. Walking, or on the train. Or on trucks taking them from the home and

'WA̱NAMPI FAMILY AT WATERHOLE' | ARTWORK BY YVONNE EDWARDS, PHOTO BY ERICA WAGNER, USED WITH PERMISSION OF DR ALAN & ELIZABETH BRISSENDEN

heartland, which many would never see again. Crying babies were carried in mothers' arms. Tearful toddlers were lifted onto fathers' shoulders. Little Yvonne, too young to understand but feeling the despair and grief, was carried to the waiting truck. Her family were sent south.

It was a turbulent day of deep distress.

The South Australian government, without consulting the A̱nangu, handed over the A̱nangu to another group of missionaries, the Lutherans who had already established a mission at Koonibba, over 300 kilometres further south-east.

So the A̱nangu were sent to the country of another Aboriginal people, land to which the A̱nangu were not related, land which the South Australian government had taken. Land which *walypala* farmers did not want because it was too hard, too harsh. Limestone land, hard and harsh under bare brown feet. So different from the soft red sand the A̱nangu had always known. Grey grey land, *pa̱na tji̱lpi* which made the A̱nangu feel *tji̱lpi*, old, old. Old and sad. Grieving for the country many of them would never see again.

Chapter Four

Maralinga

In 1951 the Australian government, which the A*n*angu knew nothing of, was secretly conferring with the British government, in a country even further away, across seas the A*n*angu had never seen or heard of, and could not begin to imagine. Without consultation with A*n*angu or warning, this Australian government gave permission to the British government for its scientists to carry out tests of their nuclear weapons – *on A*n*angu lands*.

These *walypala* did not know A*n*angu country. They had not felt its age-old rocks and its forgiving sand beneath their feet. They had not slept and dreamed under

DETAIL FROM 'MARALINGA [I]' | ARTWORK BY YVONNE EDWARDS

its stars or seen the moon rise, its silver sliver growing gradually to a golden orb, bathing the country in its lovely light. They had not heard the stir of wind and the whirr of wings in its bushes, or seen the tracks of its tiny lizards. They had not waited upon *Wanampi*, the Rainbow Serpent, to send up the precious water for their parched mouths. They had not gnawed on kangaroo tails slow cooked in glowing embers, nor sucked on mallee flowers for their sweetness. They did not know where the wild figs and the bush tomatoes grew. They had not smelled the smoke of the camp fires or the scent of rain on the grateful ground. They had not sung and danced and celebrated the country in *inmas* from time immemorial.

These *walypala* had not gnawed on kangaroo tails slow cooked in glowing embers, nor sucked on mallee flowers for their sweetness.

'WANAMPI, THE RAINBOW SERPENT' | ARTWORK BY YVONNE EDWARDS

They did not know. And they did not care.

Some *walypala* who did know, who did care and who did speak up for the A̱nangu, were ignored.

'*MA̱LU* (RED KANGAROO) AND *KA̱LAYA* (EMU)', 2009 | ARTWORK BY YVONNE EDWARDS, PHOTO BY PAM DIMENT, COURTESY OF TJUTJUNA ARTS & CULTURE CENTRE

And so a new wave of *walypala* came, sitting down on Anangu lands at a place they named Maralinga,* among the mallee and the wildflowers, the *malu* (red kangaroo) and the *kipara* (bush turkey). Bringing a different poison. An even more deadly poison than rations. Radioactive poison which would contaminate the pristine lands for 24 000 years. Radioactive poison which would bring more heartache and grief to generations of Anangu and to *walypala* too. Radioactive poison which causes disease, deformities and death. Long, slow, painful dying to Yvonne's husband and two of her sons. And other members of her family.

---

* *Maralinga* is the word for thunder from another northern Australian Aboriginal language the Anangu had never heard and did not know existed. The Anangu word for thunder is *tuuni*.

Chapter Five

Childhood – good times and bad

Yvonne's mother was Mavis Tymunee Brown and her father was Bob Giles, a *walypala* farmer near Coorabie. Her mother was young when Yvonne was born and she lived with kindly A<u>n</u>angu Martha Edwards, who cared for her and baby Yvonne.

Yvonne later had a stepfather, Tommy Murka, and two half-brothers, Colin and Ronald, and two half-sisters, Noreen and Wanda. After being moved from Ooldea, the Murka family went first to Ooldea Tank,

DETAIL FROM 'WA<u>N</u>AMPI AT WATERHOLE' | ARTWORK BY YVONNE EDWARDS

YVONNE (RIGHT) WITH HER STEPFATHER, TOMMY MURKA, HER MOTHER, MAVIS TYMUNEE BROWN AND SIBLING C. 1955-6 | (AA 827/1/60), PHOTO COURTESY OF SOUTH AUSTRALIAN MUSEUM

an old government tank at Monburu, and then on to Tjinnalumba Tank with other families. Water no longer came cool and sweet from *Wanampi*'s secret rockholes.

Yvonne remembered how the old people would wake *Wanampi* to give them water: 'Some waterholes, you know, the thing the old people talk about – the water snake. They throw a stone. Wake him up. They say, "We got no water. Can you give us some water?" Snake hears. He throws up water and they fill their kangaroo-skin bags.'

Now the water came from whitefella iron tanks catching rainwater from whitefella iron roofs, to wash clothes which whitefellas wanted Anangu to wear. Yvonne remembered those early years, when the Lutheran missionaries were in charge: 'When camp moved, we'd walk miles. Walkabout camp. We'd camp on the way, just a fire to keep us warm, no blanket. Get up early morning. Only old peoples, womens with babies taken by truck.

'When people were living in wurlies they'd go down to tank or windmill. Sit all day doing their washing in tubs. Boil big copper for water, use Velvet soap and rub clothes on rock. Probably learned that at Ooldea. No washing machines, no detergents those days. They'd bring their children, cook their lunch. Ration time every

week. Flour, tea, sugar, dripping. Sometimes clothes, pants for men, a dress and jumper for women, and a blanket for old people.'

At Middle Yard, where they camped next, the rainwater tank was underground and the women fetched water in ration buckets which had been used for dripping (fat). Yvonne described how it was done: 'Carry bucket on your head. Your neck ache and your back ache. Make a pad, a ring, out of shirt, jumper, ring for the top of your head to balance bucket on. And you walk.' She remembered how on sports days the women would run with a bucket on their heads. Yvonne was good at this, and to the end of her life she would carry boxes and packages on her head.

The missionaries organised school for the children, moving from camp to camp. 'Walkabout school. Wherever camp stopped for water, there was our school. Our first school at Ooldea Tank. Sit on ground under tree. Blackboard against tree. Sometimes canvas awning for shade. At walkabout school we had rations. School was all right but I wasn't talking good English.' She was always scared

LIFE AFTER OOLDEA IN THE 1950s: (TOP) WASHING AT CHINNALUMBA (TJINNALUMBA) WELL | [SAMA 1083/2/4/2255]; (BOTTOM) DISTRIBUTION OF RATIONS | [SAMA 1083/2/3/2166] | PHOTOS COURTESY OF SOUTH AUSTRALIAN MUSEUM

of the A̲nangu teacher, Mr Minning. He was very strict and he would smack them if they didn't listen.

WALKABOUT SCHOOL AT YALATA IN THE 1950s | [SAMA 1083/44/8727]. PHOTO COURTESY OF SOUTH AUSTRALIAN MUSEUM

Later her mother took her to Fowlers Bay to live with a kind couple, Mr and Mrs Dicks, so that she could go to school. Yvonne was an eager pupil and became fluent in English in addition to her mother tongue, Pitjantjatjara, learning to read and to write in a clear firm hand. She remembered happy times. 'When they had Easter egg hunt in the sand hills I could find them because I would follow the tracks. And I'd share with everyone. When I was staying with this couple [at Fowlers Bay], they were a nice old couple, but they had to leave.'

Then life became very unhappy for Yvonne. 'They gave me to another couple who were bad. We went to bed frightened. Man used to say, "Call me Daddy," and he used to give us stuff, trying to make us drink. Lots of glass broken there and I cut

YOUNG YVONNE IN FANCY DRESS C. 1958, FOWLERS BAY | [SAMA 1083/44/8857], PHOTO COURTESY OF SOUTH AUSTRALIAN MUSEUM

my feet. I used to be scared and watch door all night. I used to crawl through window and call out to people walking past, ask them to take me away.

'Policeman used to talk to me down jetty (when I was there with two younger ones) and say "Go home to your mother". He sent me back to Yalata on mail truck and I was happy. But no school there.

'At Yalata lots of cars would come looking for me, and the old people, they used to hide me in their wurley. And men came round with torches looking for me, and the old people would cover me with wheat bags. Then man lifted wheat bag, found me, threw me in car and locked door. Drove me back to Fowlers Bay, locked door and window of my room, and I used to watch through window, scared. Very scared.'*

Yvonne was so happy when her mother came and took her back to the Lutheran mission at Yalata: 'No houses there. Only a ration shed and caravan at first.'

YOUNG YVONNE WITH DOG C. 1958, FOWLERS BAY | [SAMA 1083/44/8858], PHOTO COURTESY OF SOUTH AUSTRALIAN MUSEUM

* Because it was government policy to remove children of mixed descent from their Aborginal families, many underwent this traumatic experience.

Chapter Six

Atom bombs on Anangu lands

Yvonne remembered growing up seeing soldiers and Land Rovers, as army personnel from Maralinga spent weekends at Yalata. 'Soldiers give oranges, apples. Sometimes played sports with us.' Always ready to see the best in people, she said, 'They were good men.'

But the men planning the atomic testing on Anangu lands they named Maralinga, had no heart, no understanding and no respect for the traditional owners. In October 1953, in weather which contravened criteria

DETAIL FROM 'MARALINGA [II]' | ARTWORK BY YVONNE EDWARDS

for safe firing, they exploded two bombs in the Totem Series at Emu Field, 320 kilometres north of Maralinga, with devastating effects on Anangu at nearby Wallatinna to the north-east.

A black mist with a metallic smell enveloped camp sites. It caused stomach pains, vomiting, choking, coughing, diarrhoea, rashes, peeling skin, headaches, and sore and running eyes. Old and frail Anangu died within days. Ten-year-old Yami Lester couldn't open his eyes and later became permanently blind.

> A black mist with a metallic smell enveloped camp sites. Old and frail Anangu died within days.

Then they commenced the Buffalo Series at Maralinga. Yvonne was just six years and 15 days old when the first bomb of 15 kilotons (15 000 tons) was detonated on 27 September 1956. The wind conditions were less than ideal, and the top of the explosion cloud rose to 11 430 metres, almost 3000 metres higher than expected, which substantially increased the range of the fallout. Over the

MUSHROOM CLOUD FROM THE ATOMIC BOMB DROPPED AT MARALINGA, 19 OCTOBER 1956 | PHOTO BY NEWS LTD/NEWSPIX

GROUND ZERO, TARANAKI, MARALINGA, SOUTH AUSTRALIA, 2011.
THE TEXT READS: WARNING ~ RADIATION HAZARD ~ RADIATION LEVELS FOR A FEW HUNDRED METRES AROUND THIS POINT MAY BE ABOVE THOSE CONSIDERED SAFE FOR PERMANENT OCCUPATION | PHOTO BY JESSIE BOYLAN

next 25 days three more bombs were detonated, totalling almost 30 kilotons (30 000 tons).

Then on 9 October 1957, when Yvonne was seven years and 27 days old, the Antler Series of three explosions culminated with the biggest bomb of all, 25 kilotons (25 000 tons). Altogether, almost 100 kilotons (100 000 tons) of explosive were dropped in the three series between 1953 and 1957. An additional series, the so-called Minor Trials, between 1953 and 1963, released almost 100 kilograms of radioactive and toxic elements, including uranium, plutonium, beryllium and a large amount of other radioactive isotopes. But no meteorological records were kept which would have indicated the spread of isotopes and contamination of the land.

> Altogether, almost 100 kilotons of explosive were dropped in the three series between 1953 and 1957.

Yvonne remembered: 'Grandfather and Grandmother telling lots of stories. They had to live at Yalata. Their home was bombed. That was their home where the bomb went off. Really frightened. They thought it was *mamu tjuta*, evil spirits, coming. Everyone was frightened, thinking about people back in the bush. Didn't know what bomb was. Later told it was poison. Parents and grandparents really wanted to go home, used to talk all the time to get their land back.'

But they were prevented by the Native Patrol Officer, Walter MacDougall.* In 1955 most of their traditional lands, named by *walypala* the Great Victoria Desert, after a British queen A̱nangu had never heard of, had been declared a Prohibited Area. Caring for country, as A̱nangu had done for millennia, was no longer possible. Forbidden. And the British *walypala* at Maralinga neither knew of nor understood the deep bond the A̱nangu had with their land. Nor did they care.

When MacDougall had tried to explain it, W.A.S. Butement, Chief Scientist, Weapons Research Establishment, wrote: 'He is apparently placing the affairs of a handful of natives above those of the British Commonwealth of Nations.'

---

* Walter MacDougall was a Native Patrol Officer appointed by the Weapons Research Establishment (W.R.E.) late in 1947 to be responsible for the welfare of all Aborigines who might be affected by the weapons testing. He was also appointed Protector of Aborigines by the South Australian Aborigines Protection Board. Although he felt genuine concern for their safety, he was expected to serve official government policy rather than A̱nangu interests.

So displaced seven-year-old Yvonne had no way of knowing how her future and that of her family would be so tragically affected. They had been made refugees.

LEFT TO RIGHT: COLIN MURKA, MARIA STEWART, RONNIE MURKA AND HARRY GIBSON AT THE LUTHERAN MISSION YALATA SIGN, 1965 | PHOTO BY DAVID CRAIG, COURTESY OF SA LUTHERAN ARCHIVES

Chapter Seven

Michael

Growing up at Yalata, Yvonne found new love. Quiet David Edwards, strong, steady, skilled in so many ways, became her trusted companion, opening the way to a long life together. David had also been born at Ooldea, on 2 August 1942, the son of Charlie and Freda Edwards, and was baptised on 24 July 1949. But when the UAM mission closed in 1952, nine-year-old David was sent south-east to the Lutheran Mission at Koonibba and placed in the Children's Home. He attended school, was confirmed, and remained at Koonibba until he was 16. When Yvonne, almost 15, and David discovered

DETAIL FROM 'TEACHING OUR CULTURE', 2007 | ARTWORK BY YVONNE EDWARDS, PHOTO BY PAM DIMENT, COURTESY OF TJUTJUNA ARTS & CULTURE CENTRE

that they were to have a child, they were thrilled, and Yvonne, always clever with her hands, took delight in making clothes for the baby, knitting a little jacket for it during the waiting months.

David and Ruth Craig remember Yvonne as a teenage schoolgirl when they both taught at Yalata A̲nangu School from 1964 to 1966. Yvonne was in the senior class under David Craig as principal, and on Saturdays

ABOVE: DAVID EDWARDS AT OOLDEA IN THE 1950S (FRONT ROW, MIDDLE) | [SAMA 1083/3/642], PHOTO COURTESY OF SOUTH AUSTRALIAN MUSEUM; FACING PAGE: EXPECTANT YVONNE, 1965 | PHOTO BY DAVID CRAIG, COURTESY OF EDWARDS FAMILY COLLECTION

she helped Ruth in the house. Only whitefella staff had houses then. A<u>n</u>angu were still living in camps. They said, 'Yvonne was very shy, never any trouble, clever, a pleasure to work with and still at school when she was pregnant. She was very musical, sang in the school choir, could harmonise by ear and was very quick at picking up

'WA<u>N</u>AMPI AT WATERHOLE' | ARTWORK BY YVONNE EDWARDS

tunes. She was the best student at drawing and in the camp men would get her to draw *malu* (red kangaroo) on boomerangs, which they would then incise.'

When the time came, on 10 August 1965, she gave birth, not in the private world of the bush surrounded by women she knew and trusted, but in a town, in a hospital, attended by *walypala* nurses she did not know. Yvonne and David were overjoyed that their firstborn was a son and they named him Michael.

But joy soon turned to grief.

The young mother was told to sign a form. She thought it was to give permission to have the baby immunised. She wrote her name on the crisp white paper. Baby Michael must have the best chance in life, protected against whitefella diseases. Measles and whooping cough and influenza had already ravaged her people.

Too late the whitefella staff in their uniforms told her as they took her brown-skinned baby. They were the Welfare. The Welfare! It was the name dreaded by Aboriginal people everywhere.[*] Breaking up families. Bringing heartbreak and loss. The paper she had signed

---

[*] As it was government policy to remove children of mixed descent, Aboriginal people feared the police and Welfare.

gave permission for him to be removed. Removed from the parents who loved him. Removed from his immediate family. Removed from his extended family of grandfathers, *tjamu*, grandmothers, *kapali*, aunts and uncles and cousins. Removed from his community. Losing his mother tongue, Pitjantjatjara. Losing the story of his people, his displaced people. Displaced himself. Into whitefella society. It was government policy. And nobody could argue with the government. Least of all Aboriginal people.

They were the Welfare.
The Welfare! It was the name dreaded
by Aboriginal people everywhere.

The whitefella government which had stolen Anangu land for atomic bombs. The whitefella government whose members and officials knew nothing about Aboriginal kinship systems and extended families. Or if they did, chose to think that nuclear families were better. The whitefella officials who did not understand or care that many arms were waiting outstretched at Yalata to embrace this precious child, to grow him up knowing his place in Anangu society.

So now baby Michael was to go to another family. A whitefella family.

Yvonne thrust the little jacket, the little jacket she had knitted with such love and hope, at the nurse who now held her precious baby son. 'He must have this. Michael must know his mother loved him,' she begged. The cold white ward echoed with her wails as the nurse carried the tiny infant away. And Yvonne's anguish never left her.

For the next 20 years Yvonne grieved for Michael and wanted to find him.

Chapter Eight

Marriage and Maralinga

Yvonne and David were married in the Church of Our Redeemer at the Koonibba Lutheran Mission on 24 July 1967 and had a long and happy marriage. They went on to have seven more children – Patrick, Jamie, Duane, Teddy, Judy, Terence and Aaron, all of whom they managed to keep. And they loved them all dearly.

Both David and Yvonne were hard workers and travelled together around the district and up to 300 kilometres beyond, doing seasonal work on *walypala*

DETAIL FROM 'MARALINGA' | ARTWORK BY YVONNE EDWARDS

PHOTO COLLAGE OF THE EDWARDS FAMILY | PHOTO BY JESSIE BOYLAN, COURTESY OF EDWARDS FAMILY COLLECTION

'properties' – building fences and stockyards, installing tanks, maintaining windmills and pipelines, shepherding and shearing, driving tractors, and stump picking on land cleared of scrub for growing pasture. Proudly independent, they would turn their hands to any job to earn money to support their family.

So in 1974 when the newly formed Yalata Community Council was granted salvage rights at Maralinga, David, an experienced tractor driver, was pleased to be chosen for the salvage team. Several temporary and ineffective 'clean-ups' had already been done. The second, Operation Brumby, in 1966, was done after the British moved out, but insufficient topsoil was used, and complete records of burial pits of contaminated material were not made. The *walypala* project manager asked the South Australian Health Department if radiation levels at the site were safe for humans and was assured there was no cause for concern. But no record of this correspondence now exists and six containers of plutonium fragments remained in concrete pits at the cemetery until 1978.

Yvonne said, 'Couldn't take womens there first. But my husband went to help. Second trip they said it was all right for womens.' So David and Yvonne moved to Maralinga with two of their young children, Duane and Teddy.

Yvonne remembers: 'When we were looking after the place at Maralinga, three or four Anangu men came to stay to help pull buildings down. When mens were at work, all the ladies used to go to the big hall and we'd jump on the big table and we'd play snooker.

'The hall had everything in it. Big kitchen with everything, plates, saucepans. We took lots back to the community at Yalata. Probably all the big bosses sat in the big flash room. All the soldiers had their meals and drinks in the bar. And everything just left there – knives, forks, glasses still on the table, pictures still hanging on the wall. One big shed, store shed was full of grey blankets, sheets and pillows. We said, "We should take some of this to the community." We took blankets and pillows to give to the old people. One weekend we put everything on truck, took it back to Yalata. Gave it to the old people and the young people. Plenty for everyone. Now when I look back and I always think about it. Why didn't someone tell us it was dangerous? When the old people covered themselves with the blankets they were breathing in that dust.

'Then some of us ladies walked around. We went into every house and checked it out – doors all open. It was a real ghost town, dingoes roaming around everywhere. I had a little dingo pup. But it died. One of the women, her baby died.

'We stayed in a dormitory near the hospital. They made part into a kitchen for us and we kept all our food in the hospital. Whitefellas stayed in the hospital. The

ON THE ROAD TO MARALINGA, 2014 | PHOTO BY JESSIE BOYLAN

pastor came up every fortnight to have a service with us outside. The church was really lovely – organ, altar, everything. We'd go and sit down, look at the hymn books. But we never used the church. Lovely gardens and flowers growing. We'd stand there to have our photo taken.

'We went to the airstrip. It's a BIG airstrip. A really big sign: Maralinga International Airport. Drive along, "This where helicopters land. And this is where the big planes land." Little bushes alongside and big buildings. A lot of rabbits because no one was there, and we chased the rabbits around Maralinga International Airport. Every afternoon we'd go down and dig for rabbits, or take a spotlight at night.

'All the ladies go for *maku* (witchetty grubs), digging them out of the ground. Walk, get lots, plenty there. Good soft sand for cooking *maku*. We were going every road, lots of roads there and we followed every road. But no trees anywhere. No grass. All dead. Then we driving around in evening and we could see the turkeys (*kipara*) sitting down on hill because there's no trees. And we cooked *kipara* near where the bombs went off, on the same road where dead wood was.

'We were driving around in Land Rovers, me and some other ladies. Land Rovers left there. We went to Watson to get things, fresh meat and vegies from the tea and sugar train once a week. Then if we see *malu* (red kangaroo) or *kalaya* (emu), we'd kill them and eat them, cook them in the ashes and share with all the other workers. Aboriginal people always share.

'I think back now, there's a lot of places I've been I shouldn't have. Nobody told us anything about it. Why didn't they tell us? Husbands working so we went back there. Took our children. We thought it was safe. But it wasn't safe. Whitefellas – they didn't tell us. Why didn't they tell us?

> **NOTICE**
> **COMMONWEALTH OF AUSTRALIA**
> **PROHIBITED AREA**
> THIS AREA HAS BEEN DECLARED A PROHIBITED AREA UNDER SECTION 8 OF THE DEFENCE (SPECIAL UNDERTAKINGS) ACT, 1952. A PERSON SHALL NOT BE IN, ENTER, OR FLY OVER THIS PROHIBITED AREA WITHOUT PROPER AUTHORIZATION.
> PENALTY:- IMPRISONMENT FOR SEVEN YEARS.
> RANGE COMMANDER • MARALINGA
> DEFACEMENT OF THIS NOTICE IS PUNISHABLE BY LAW.

IN 1955 MOST OF THE GREAT VICTORIA DESERT WAS DECLARED A PROHIBITED AREA | [SAMA 1083/4/729]. PHOTO COURTESY OF SOUTH AUSTRALIAN MUSEUM

'Mima Smart came after, then Martha Edwards, Margaret May came later.'

Mima Smart came with her husband, Yvonne's brother, Colin Murka. Mima said, 'Didn't think about danger. Thought it was a good place, a safe place because there was a church at the end of the street. Made me feel happy. Thought it was home.'

Yvonne said, 'My husband and I stayed longest. I had children with me, Teddy not quite one, and Duane about two. When the mens go out from village to pull down shed at Kittens [one of the Minor Trials sites], bitumens everywhere and sheds everywhere. Lots of sheds. Whitefellas wanted to buy sheds, church, big hall. Came from all over. Buildings went everywhere [across South Australia and beyond]. I'd sit down by dead tree and make a fire, cook dinner for A̲nangu workers. Went home when they knock off. Made a big fire near heap, sit down and yarn, and listen to dingoes. At warm nights we'd sit on top of big dry swimming pool on hill, lovely and cool, fresh air, calm, really quiet. And we could see all the lights of train and houses in Watson.

'We followed bitumen road to place where bomb went off and we were all standing there looking – a BIG hole with a big fence around it and NO TREES FOR

MILES, no green leaves, JUST DEAD TREES, lots of dead animals. No kangaroos. North wind blowing where bomb went off. Still hot. We were walking in bare feet

ROCKHOLES, ON THE ROAD TO MARALINGA, 2014 | PHOTO BY JESSIE BOYLAN

looking around. Nobody told us we should wear shoes. We went to have a look. We thought it was safe. But it wasn't. We went back to village, told whitefellas. They said, "You shouldn't have been there." But nobody told us.

> 'We thought it was safe. But it wasn't safe. Whitefellas – they didn't tell us. Why didn't they tell us?'

Mima Smart said, 'Nobody told us we should wear shoes. Nobody told us it was dangerous. It's not good to live there now, or put camps up for the old people. That place is damaged. Nobody would like to live there now. Told now that radiation still on that ground. But we don't know yet if we've got that sickness.'

Yvonne remembered: 'When we went back we saw this BIG crack in the ground. We dug out this crack with front-end loader – and there was new washing machines still in their boxes, fridges, Land Rovers, motorbikes – just covered over.

'Mens were itchy from pulling buildings down, scratching all night. Later came out in sores all over their chests. I seen the men working trying to cover drums over, full of poison. Whitefellas all had masks and protective clothing. White boots, gloves, hoods, goggles, overalls. But none for A̱nangu. A̱nangu men had nothing. My husband just had ordinary clothes and they made him drive front-end loader to bring drums of poison. They should have told him what it was. They should have given him something to put over his mouth. He had to dig the holes to bury the drums, all the dust blowing up. North wind blowing. No mask. Driving front-end loader to cover plutonium and put cement over it. Aboriginal fella getting all the dust on top of front-end loader. They should have told my husband what it was. That was really poison they were working on that day. We could see them working there. A̱nangu men worked without protective clothing. Weren't given protective clothing.'

The late Mabel Queama, whose husband also has died, said, 'We walked to Taranaki [bomb site]. We been there. Couldn't sleep that night. Coughing all night. Coughing, coughing, coughing. Couldn't walk much. Now everyone at Oak Valley has breathing problems. All the old people. Everyone has puffers. My lungs no good.'

'We stayed longest,' Yvonne said. 'I stayed, later with three small children. But we didn't know the place was

YVONNE AND DAVID EDWARDS WITH THEIR YOUNGEST CHILDREN (LEFT TO RIGHT): TERENCE, YVONNE, AARON, DAVID AND JUDY

dangerous, poisoned. One of our sons, Teddy, got very sick. He was just a baby. He was taken back to Yalata and later to Adelaide because he was still sick. My husband got sick later, couldn't see properly. His eyes. Died of lung cancer, spreading fast. Cancer all over his lungs.

'All A<u>n</u>angu mens who worked at Maralinga finished now. Lost a sister too from cancer. In her 20s. And an uncle in his 40s from cancer. And an auntie from cancer. Two of my sons died in their 40s from cancer. Sometimes I cry at night. Used to be a lot of old people. But not now. Used to have a lot of old people when we first came from Ooldea. But only a few now. Nobody over 60 now. A big centre for old people at Oak Valley. But not many left. Only Alice Cox and Margaret May. All our people end up in cemetery because of that bomb. It destroyed our old people. I cry at night – for my mother, grandmothers, aunties.'

In 2010 Yvonne, who had just turned 60, said, 'I don't know why I'm still alive. I went everywhere [at Maralinga]. Everywhere I shouldn't have. Nobody told us. Not good to live there now. That place is damaged. You can't fix that. You can go for a visit. But you can't live there. Nobody would like to live there now.'

Chapter Nine

Refugees, prisoners, and rebuilders of community

Forcibly removed from their red desert sand country, often hot but always forgiving under their bare feet, the A<u>n</u>angu found themselves confined. Confined to the country of another ancient people, a country with a different story. Where the cold wind from the sea they had never known whistling through the boughs of their *wiltjas* (shelters) chilled their hearts as well as their

DETAIL FROM PAINTING INSPIRED BY KANGAROO ENTRAILS | ARTWORK BY YVONNE EDWARDS, PHOTO BY ERICA WAGNER, IN THE COLLECTION OF CHRISTOBEL MATTINGLEY

bodies. Resettled on country that whitefella farmers did not want because they could not make the stony ground yield crops.

The A<u>n</u>angu grieved for their lost country, its secret places, its sacred sites. They worried for its ancient waters guarded by *Wa<u>n</u>ampi* from time immemorial. They had no links to this land to which they had been so suddenly and so forcibly removed. This land they were prevented from leaving each time they tried. They had no roots in its hard pale earth. They said it was *pana tjilpi*. They said it made them *tjilpi*, old. They were desolate among the grey humps and hummocks of its saltbush and its spindly-stemmed eucalypts domed in dull green. They wanted to go home. The grandmothers and grandfathers said, 'We want to go back to where we were nice and peaceful. Yalata is not our home.'

Martha Edwards said, 'They kicked us out of Ooldea.'

Mima Smart said, 'People wanted to go home. To show the children where family come from, where their country was, to show them their Dreamings, to show them the rockholes, and how they travelled from rockhole to rockhole. Their children were looking forward to going home.'

Yvonne said, 'People suffered a lot when the bomb

went off. People didn't like Yalata. They were used to the red sand. This ground's white, making us old.'

Within a few decades after the missionaries' arrival at Ooldea the independent A<u>n</u>angu way of life had been eroded, drastically changed to whitefella dependence. Caring for country was impossible. Generations were robbed of their ancestral responsibilities. Links with the land were replaced by the activities of Lutheran missionaries. People no longer slept with their dogs by campfires under the stars. Gradually houses replaced *wiltjas* and *wurlies* (shelters). Angles and straight lines replaced curves. Doors, windows. Tables, chairs. Taps, cupboards. Cars, 4WDs. Petrol. Hunting and gathering further superseded, not only by rations, but by the introduction of money. Money to be exchanged at a store for more whitefella foods in cans and packets and plastic bags. And later – most devastating of all – in bottles and flagons. Grog.

With the introduction of drinking rights for Aboriginal people in 1965, some A<u>n</u>angu began to turn to alcohol to blunt their pain, their loss, their longing, to blot out their grief at losing their homelands. And unscrupulous whitefellas exploited this anguish.

After the missionaries withdrew in 1975, Yalata became

MAKING ARTEFACTS: (ABOVE) DAVID WAS NOTED FOR CARVING KANGAROOS; (FACING PAGE) YVONNE LOVED MAKING DIDGERIDOOS INCISED WITH TRADITIONAL DESIGNS | COURTESY OF EDWARDS FAMILY COLLECTION

a self-governing community and Yvonne and David, who shared a deep faith, worked hard to make the community succeed, always ready to be where they were needed, nurturing tradition, fostering culture, organising hunting and fishing trips and youth camps, assisting with the roadhouse and the store. Both served on the Community Council as chairpersons and as members. David, quiet and unassuming, became first manager of the Tullawon

Health Service, which he continued to serve for over 30 years, travelling to India and New Zealand to research health issues. He also established the valuable link with the Royal Flying Doctor Service, arranging for visits to Yalata.

Eve Dobbins, office manager of the Yalata Community Council for four years, said, 'Yvonne was a very strong lady. The community always came first with her. She wanted the best for them, always advocating that people should move forward. Without forgetting their own cultural side, she wanted to interact with wider society.'

Both David and Yvonne worked in the school to assist whitefella staff to better understand the students and their backgrounds. In 1979, Yvonne, with Maureen Kugena and Marjorie Sandimar, compiled an illustrated booklet in English, *Yalata/story*, for the South Australian Education Department, and in 1986 Yvonne did another booklet in English, *Collecting Maku/story*, published by the Yalata Aboriginal School Literacy Centre.

Grant Fiedler, a former principal of Yalata Anangu School, said, 'Yvonne always made me feel very welcome by allowing me to sit with her and by giving her time to talk with me and listen to whatever I had to say. In the conversations we had she made me feel respected, when in fact all I was trying to do was to show her how much I respected her and the people she represented.'

David also served for ten years on the Wangka Wilurrara Regional Council, campaigning for recognition of Anangu rights to land, and as an Aboriginal and Torres Strait Islander Commission (ATSIC) representative, fighting for respect for arts, culture, heritage, language and men's issues. Yvonne was one of three women appointed in 1997 to the new Wangka Wilurrara Women's Advisory Committee, organising a regional forum to discuss women's issues. She was a founding member of the Yalata Women's Choir and travelled with it to Western Australia to give concerts. Short and sturdy, she was also a keen netball player in the Yalata team's early days. David also loved sport. Well built and exceptionally tall, fondly known as Long David, he played football in both the Yalata and Koonibba teams, and later supported and encouraged younger players.

Pastor Deane Heyne said, 'David's life traversed a time in the life of the community when cultural and lifestyle changes came thick and fast, bringing some

YVONNE (FRONT RIGHT, WEARING THE LETTER C) PLAYED IN THE YALATA NETBALL TEAM, 1991 | PHOTO BY MICHELE MADIGAN

positives for the people but also allowing some new practices to introduce unknown and unwanted suffering for the people. David made himself available to deal with issues in his community, bringing some successes, despite the frustrations that accompany being in leadership positions. He put much into life, on the football field, his family, travel overseas, and his face-to-face encounters with organisations that sought to right the wrongs placed on his people.'

With dismay, Yvonne and David observed the damage that alcohol was inflicting on their depressed and dispirited community. They organised bush camps, taking drinkers away from alcohol, reviving old skills making artefacts and bush medicine, hunting and gathering, eating bush tucker, renewing pride in self sufficiency, rebuilding community. They worked for many years to try to prevent the sale of alcohol at roadhouses at Nundroo, only 47 kilometres away from Yalata, and Nullarbor and Penong along the Eyre Highway, and to counteract the effects of grog and drugs brought into Yalata. The sealing of the road to Ceduna, almost 200 kilometres east, also facilitated access to alcohol.

The elders campaigned tirelessly for the return of their lands and in 1984 an Act of Parliament, the

Maralinga Tjarutja Land Rights Act, gave the displaced people rights over their own land. The ceremony on 18 December 1984 in the bush near Maralinga was a great celebration, when Premier Bannon handed over the title deed granting freehold rights to 76 420 square kilometres to the traditional owners through the newly constituted

TOMMY QUEAMA AND JACK BAKER WITH THE TITLE TO MARALINGA TJARUTJA LANDS, 18 DECEMBER 1984 | PHOTO BY MILTON WORDLEY/NEWSPIX

body, Maralinga Tjarutja. The old people who had travelled over that land, who knew it from the soles of their feet up through every fibre of their bodies, every corner of their hearts and minds, were happy once more. Old ladies were crying with joy. Now, at last, after over 30 years they were going home. Home. To the spinifex country and the red sand.

> Now, at last, after over 30 years
> they were going home.

A jubilant group, over 80 men, women and children, set out for the country from which they had been banned through three decades of heartache, visiting many places before settling down to make their home at Oak Valley. Oak Valley, where the graceful desert oaks grow in groves and the sand rolls in undulating hills and valleys to the far horizon. Oak Valley, where the wide night sky glitters with myriads of stars. Stars and space telling their own stories as they change with the seasons. Stories dear to the hearts of A<u>n</u>angu.

Some people, including the Edwards family, chose to remain at Yalata. They thought it was too dangerous to go back. They feared that their lands had been poisoned

YALATA COMMUNITY SIGN | PHOTO BY DANIELLE MARWICK

by the bombs. They feared they might get sick. Mima Smart said, 'We want to see Yalata go forward. We want it to be a better place for the children.' So Yvonne and David and others, although still yearning for their own country, worked hard to put down roots in the pale stony earth at Yalata for their children and their children's children.

> Aaron said, 'It's her [my mother's] life story, trying to stop alcohol and drugs.' To the end of her life, Yvonne continued to campaign against alcohol, petrol sniffing and drugs.

On Good Friday, 1991, five Yalata people were killed in a horrific road accident, which traumatised the community. Another appeal by the Council to the Licensing Court was finally granted a hearing in December, and Yvonne, together with a large group from Yalata, drove 1000 kilometres to Adelaide to attend Court on 19 December. The judge ruled that no full-strength alcohol was to be sold from Nundroo, Nullarbor and Penong to Yalata residents for off-premises consumption, but light beer could be. After 16 years of fighting the scourge remained.*

So elders continued to campaign for tighter restrictions. *Maru wiya*. No grog. In 1995 Yvonne Edwards, Henry Beard, Sandra Bridley and Heather York wrote to the Liquor Commissioner:

---

* By 1978 the number of deaths each year at Yalata was higher than births, and the birth rate continued to drop while the death rate rose. In the decade between 1972 and 1982, 29 deaths were alcohol-related, almost a third of all in the community. Between 1986 and 1991, 15 people died in alcohol-related road accidents.

All the people who have been living here all their lives, the sober people – we'll just move out if they get drink back here. We'll be moving out – taking all our children. We don't want the wine here. We don't want to go back. We want to go forward.

When the wine/drink here from the takeaway – people were hurt here. We lose a lot of people – accidents on the road. People come back – drink on the side of the road. Get run over. When drinking was here kids were frightened. Couldn't sleep at night. Kids too tired to go to school. Got no money for food and clothes.

People won't be working properly in the office or clinic. People will be coming there smashing windows, throwing stones also. That's true. *Tjukur mulapa*. That's a true story. The lady in Penong [hotel keeper] just wants to make money. She doesn't care about people getting bashed up, losing their lives.

Aaron said, 'It's her [my mother's] life story, trying to stop alcohol and drugs.' To the end of her life, Yvonne continued to campaign against alcohol, petrol sniffing and drugs.

Chapter Ten

Yvonne the artist

Yvonne also helped establish the Women's Centre, encouraging women to develop their skills in art and craft, producing work to sell. She herself loved carving birds and making didgeridoos beautifully incised with traditional designs. Both she and David were also noted for carving kangaroos from quandong and *gudia*, Western myall, with its lovely contrast of light and dark wood. Rita Bryant described the patient process, which required many hours of work. 'Chop down *gudia*. Carve out shape with hatchet. Mouse, bird, wombat. Rub it down with rasp. Rub it, rub it. Smooth it with sandpaper. Smooth it,

DETAIL FROM 'WA<u>N</u>AMPI AND WATERHOLES' | ARTWORK BY YVONNE EDWARDS, PHOTO BY PAM DIMENT, COURTESY OF TJUTJUNA ARTS & CULTURE CENTRE

smooth it, smooth it. Then make eyes, nose.'

When it was predicted that the best place to view Halley's Comet in 1986 would be Ceduna, Yvonne and others showed initiative and enterprise, organising a working group to make artefacts to sell to visitors coming from all over the world. In 1999 Yvonne received a unique commission to make a *kuturu*, a stick used only by senior women as a symbol of leadership. Under the guidance of her grandmother, highly respected elder Rene Sandimar, Yvonne crafted this rare piece. It was presented in a ceremony featuring the elements of fire and water to Sister Mary Cresp, to help empower her as Leader of the Sisters of St Joseph, a Roman Catholic order which supports A̱nangu and other Aboriginal peoples.

To encourage self-sufficiency and pride, Yvonne, David and others had taken the initiative in building Yalata Roadhouse, opened in the 1970s as a sales outlet for the artworks created by community members.

TOP: YVONNE WITH HER ARTWORKS AT THE PORT LINCOLN DESERT TO DUNES ART EXHIBITION OPENING, MARCH 2010 | PHOTO BY PAM DIMENT; ABOVE: THE *KUTURU* YVONNE WAS COMMISSIONED TO MAKE IN 1999 | IMAGE USED WITH PERMISSION OF TRUSTEES OF THE SISTERS OF ST JOSEPH; OVERLEAF: *GUDIA* (WESTERN MYALL), USED FOR CARVING ARTEFACTS | PHOTO BY BILL DOWLING

When it was forced to close in 2006 because of asbestos in the structure, the Ceduna Aboriginal Arts and Cultural Centre became the showcase for their work. Director Pam Diment had great respect and admiration for Yvonne. 'Yvonne was a very strong woman. An incredibly strong, strong woman. She had so much talent. I admired her skill. As a teacher and an artist you couldn't get a better person. She was always willing to talk about culture. She'd answer any questions. She was always willing to talk about her art. Her connection to country, story line was so strong, it always came out in her work. And she had so much knowledge. She was always willing to pass it on. She had a passion for teaching people. I wish she had had a place where she could have worked. She had so many obstacles in her life, and was under so many pressures.'

In painting, Yvonne had discovered a new joy and a new skill. She was a natural artist, although she did not see herself as such. 'I'm not really a painter. But I like doing some stories. Just putting my story into a painting for people to look at, just like I'm telling a story, but it's in the painting.'

'SEVEN SISTERS' (TOP) | COURTESY OF TULLAWON HEALTH SERVICE, YALATA AND 'NATIVITY' (BOTTOM) | COURTESY OF EDWARDS FAMILY | ARTWORKS BY YVONNE EDWARDS, PHOTOS BY JESSIE BOYLAN

'WANAMPI AND WATERHOLES' | ARTWORK BY YVONNE EDWARDS, PHOTO BY PAM DIMENT, COURTESY OF TJUTJUNA ARTS & CULTURE CENTRE

Bob Sim, Principal of Yalata A<u>n</u>angu School, said, 'Yvonne was able to share many important stories through her paintings and those stories have travelled far. I am sure she has inspired many other A<u>n</u>angu artists in Yalata, women especially, to also use art to convey their thoughts and stories to others.'

Transferring her world with paint onto canvas, Yvonne created pictures of what she knew and loved, and of what she knew and feared. She worked quickly and deftly, with an unerring sense of proportion and design, often creating borders or backgrounds in fine dot painting patterns to frame objects, faces or symbolic scenes. Some of these major works adorn the walls of the Tullawon Health Service rooms at Yalata. Bush tucker and *Wa<u>n</u>ampi*, the Rainbow Serpent, were favourite subjects. She also created scenes of human action and interaction, some almost in a comic strip style to engage the viewer, though the subjects, the effects of alcohol and the atomic tests, were far from comic.

'I'm not really a painter. But I like doing some stories. Just putting my story into a painting for people to look at, just like I'm telling a story, but it's in the painting.'

'BUSH TUCKER' SHOWING GUM BLOSSOMS, WITCHETTY GRUBS, LIZARDS, EGGS AND GATHERERS WITH THEIR DIGGING STICKS | ARTWORK BY YVONNE EDWARDS, COURTESY OF BEV FIRTH AND ANDREW MOORE

She described the painting shown overleaf: 'The bomb went off (central image). The soldiers going through Yalata all the time (top left). Mens in uniforms and drums of poison (bottom left). This where all our old people end up in the cemetery from the bomb. That poison, it destroyed all our old people (top right). Here the people are sad. They went back to the land, and they're sitting down, sad, because it's not the same like it was before – that land (bottom right).' Yvonne did a similar painting, reproduced as a poster, in an effort to raise awareness of the devastation caused by the British nuclear tests.

Painting became a way of life, a way of exploring the past, celebrating the present in colours which shouted and sang, in patterns which danced and wove their way across canvases large and small, in stories and symbols. Over three decades her work would evoke admiration and give new understanding to a whitefella generation beginning to learn about and appreciate Anangu culture.

OVERLEAF: 'MARALINGA [II]' | ARTWORK BY YVONNE EDWARDS

Chapter Eleven

Mother to many – caring and sharing

Yvonne was a small lady with a very big heart. Warm, generous, caring and always sharing, she earned the respect and affection of her community and many in the wider world. She loved children and children loved her. She gave them the love and nurture that sometimes their own grog-affected families could not give. She looked after petrol sniffers, taking them on 'sniffers camps', where she and other elders would engage them in hunting, making artefacts, and learning about their

DETAIL FROM 'TEACHING OUR CULTURE', 2007, SHOWING GROUPS OF YOUNGER PEOPLE WITH AN ELDER. TOP LEFT AND BOTTOM RIGHT GROUPS WITH WIND BREAKS | ARTWORK BY YVONNE EDWARDS, PHOTO BY PAM DIMENT, COURTESY OF TJUTJUNA ARTS & CULTURE CENTRE

culture, yarning as they walked or sat down beside the campfire.

For sorry camps she used to cook all the breakfasts and dinners. As dawn was just breaking, she used to be up stoking and feeding the fires, kettles on, porridge bubbling away. It was still misty and fresh, and the smell of the bush and smoke from the fire was soothing. 'Best time of the day,' Yvonne would say. Later she would go round collecting money for the food, making sure that everyone paid their share. 'She was our backbone,' Eileen Miller declared.

Yvonne's daughter Judy remembered, 'Always helping people. A lot of people came down for a Christian conference in Yalata. A big wind that day. Fire going and fire burned all the blankets. She went to see store manager and asked for blankets and mattresses and he helped.'

Josie MacArthur, Yvonne's sister Aboriginal way, who spent many years with her, said, 'She was a great inspiration to everyone. She did lots and lots of things, especially for old people and kids. People would come to her with their troubles. She cared for her nephew Desmond Tschuna after his parents died when he was a child. He was like another son to her. When she was chairperson of the Council she spoke up to get funding for the community. White people respected her, loved her too.'

Yvonne enjoyed nothing more than taking children, *tjitji tjuta*, out bush, teaching them the skills she had learned and practised, traditional hunting and camping, looking for bush tucker, sharing her wide knowledge of bush medicine with them. With the help of Michele Madigan, she and Brenda Day shared some of this knowledge in *Going for Kalta: hunting for sleepy lizards at Yalata*, published in 1997 by Jukurrpa Books, IAD Press. This book won the Children's Book Council of Australia Award for non-fiction in 1998.

OVERLEAF: IMAGES FROM *GOING FOR KALTA: HUNTING FOR SLEEPY LIZARDS AT YALATA* | COURTESY OF IAD PRESS

'Where's that sleepy lizard? You can't see that *kalta*. He's hiding inside the bush. But you can see the track. When you find his track, then you can find him. Look! There he is!' Yvonne hits the *kalta* against the *punu*, the wood, she hits his *kata*, his head – against the *punu*. She kills that sleepy lizard. Then she pulls its tail and pulls its head – she makes sure it's dead. Yvonne's ready now to take those *kalta* back to the camp fire. Brenda cleans the *kalta*, takes out the stomach and dung, but leaves the liver and lungs, before she puts the *kalta* on the fire which has gone down. She moves away the coals and makes the ground soft and puts the *kalta* in the soft part. She turns the coals with a stick; she makes that *kalta* warm. She covers it with the last of the coals. Yvonne puts sand on so the sleepy lizard doesn't get burned; it gets nice and juicy inside. *Kuka palya!* Good meat!'*

Always observant, Yvonne also loved watching the skinks in a friend's garden in Adelaide. She had an enquiring mind and thought about what she saw. 'That one – he mens. See him chasing that one – that one

---

* Text from *Going for Kalta: hunting for sleepy lizards at Yalata* (courtesy of IAD Press).

womans.' And she would chuckle as the bigger lizard darted after the smaller one across the warm path. She always looked hopefully too for koalas, occasionally to be seen in nearby gum trees.

In *Maralinga: The Anangu Story*, Yvonne described the new skill developed at Monburu after her people had been removed from Ooldea. Here they found another source of *kuka palya*, good meat – *watu*, wombats which lived in the limestone country. 'Three or four ladies

YVONNE AND FRIENDS HUNTING FOR *WATU*, WOMBATS, AT KOORINGABIE, MARCH 2008 | PHOTOS BY PAM DIMENT

would go with their dogs for *watu*. "Here's a nice hole." They had a little tool. Wire. Just dig, dig, dig. Hole getting deeper. She'd tell the other lady, "Dig over there. That's where he might come out." They'd have no dinner. They'd make fire and sleep overnight. No blankets. Cover the hole over so that the wombat couldn't get out. Hard ground. DEEP hole.

'Next day dig, dig, dig. Put a long stick in. Can sometimes see hair on end of stick and they say, "It's there!" Push the crowbar in, pull him out. Cut wombat up, put him on their head, climb over dog fence, night time. Wombats go mangy in winter eating fresh grass. Don't eat them in winter. No water, dry grass and they go fat in summer.'

Yvonne said, 'When we're travelling, in bush or just sitting down long way from shop, we share. Even when we have very little we share tucker with people who have nothing. Share water too. So next day none of us have anything.' If Yvonne had had a motto, it would have been 'care and share'.

Val Surch, former co-ordinator of the Women's Centre, said, 'Yvonne Edwards was a leader. She was a calm person, always in control. She constantly thought about how to help her family and community. She showed

BUSHLAND AROUND YALATA, 2014 | PHOTO BY JESSIE BOYLAN

YVONNE | PHOTO BY SUE McGOVERN

such insight into how others felt and what they needed. She was bossy in a way that made us all want to obey and please her. She loved to tell stories and give advice. She had incredible strength of character and walked as though she knew a lot more than she could see. When she was worried she would giggle. When she was happy she laughed from her belly.'

Val described a special farewell camp Yvonne organised for her when she was leaving. '"Come on, we get [kangaroo] tails, make damper out there in the bush! I take you to a nice place, we sit." Yvonne gathered two carloads of women and another eight arrived to travel in the troopy.* Yvonne took us to a beautiful place where huge *maireanas* (saltbush) were flowering. "Here good place," she said, got out and sat. She motioned me to sit also. Then the orders started and everyone obeyed the respected elder. Wood was collected, fires lit, damper made. At the last camp I'd told her that burning the plastic bags of rubbish could cause cancer and harm the birds. She then yelled to the women, "Don't burn that, give you kensa [cancer]." She was obeyed, no question. Such respect. I wondered what would happen this time.

'It was so warm and quiet I dozed off. Her words, "Make tea, then we go," woke me. Kettles on, she started her speech.

'"Val she goin'. She show us things and we don't forget. When we pass here we say, "That's where we sit with Val. Make damper, cook tails. She shows us things in the bush. She knows birds and what grows. We remember."

---

* A troopy is a Toyota LandCruiser Troop Carrier.

'Everyone was quiet, thinking, smiling, nodding. Slowly the women stood, gathered all the rubbish and put it in the back of the troopy. Yvonne nudged me, "For you," she said.'

The Edwards were a close family. Yvonne's children and their partners and children have paid tributes to how she cared for them. Duane, Teddy, Judy, Terence and Aaron said of their mother, 'You will stay within family hearts. You'll live on within generations forever. If we can be as special as you, your work as a mother was done and will grow.' Her son-in-law and daughters-in-law said, 'You showed us and taught us many things which we hope to give to our children's children.'

> In A̲nangu society, cousins are called sisters and brothers.

Her 17 grandchildren and her great-grandson said about their nanna, 'You taught us to love and share, always to care for our loved ones everywhere. You always protected us throughout our life, taught us hunting, fishing, camping, and singing songs at night, fire always burning bright, sharing stories all night.'

YVONNE WITH TERENCE (LEFT), AARON (FRONT RIGHT), JOY WEST AND SON BEHIND, YALATA, 1992 | PHOTO BY MICHELE MADIGAN

Matthew Kelly, one of the many young people who benefited from Yvonne's nurture, also has warm memories. He remembered how Yvonne cared for him when he was told by Pastor Heyne that his mother had cancer. From school in Adelaide he caught the bus to Port Augusta, where he found Yvonne waiting for him at the bus stop to take him straightaway to the hospital to see his mother. He said, 'She always made me feel good.'

> Yvonne was a small lady with a very big heart. She loved children and children loved her.

Another young person for whom she also cared, said, 'Forever ringing and yarning, checking up and laughing, she always made me smile…She made me who I am.' Others said, 'She taught me so many things. Writing and saying would never be enough.'

Pastor Bryce Clark, whose ministry at Ferryden Park St Paul's Lutheran Church embraced Anangu, came

TOP: YVONNE LOVED TAKING CHILDREN OUT BUSH AND TEACHING THEM TRADITIONAL SKILLS | PHOTO BY PAM DIMENT; BOTTOM LEFT: YVONNE HOLDING BRENTON SANDIMAR, OUTSIDE PORT AUGUSTA HOSPITAL | PHOTO BY MICHELE MADIGAN; BOTTOM RIGHT: YVONNE AND JUDY, 1982 | PHOTO BY JAN WILLSMORE

BASKET-MAKING WORKSHOP AT YALATA C. 2006–8: YVONNE (FRONT LEFT), VAL SURCH (FRONT RIGHT), JOSIE MACARTHUR (FAR LEFT) AND LEANNE COX (TOP RIGHT) | PHOTO BY RITA BRYANT

to know Yvonne well after she moved to Adelaide and remembered her as a strong-minded, principled person. 'She knew what was right and what was wrong.'

Judy Clark said, 'She was a very special person to me and I admired her greatly. While being an obviously proud Anangu woman, she was able to cross cultural divides. She seemed just as comfortable, familiar and able working within Western culture and advocating for her people, especially the young girls, as she did within her Anangu culture.

'We met Yvonne in 1998 when she and Mima Smart came to Adelaide for the Franklin Graham Crusade. They and about 20 other folk from Yalata stayed at our place, camping on the back verandah. At the time, my husband Bryce was at Seminary and I worked to support the family. I remember clearly being called into the kitchen and sitting around the table with Bryce, Yvonne and Mima, and all of a sudden being given a wad of money by the ladies to assist with expenses. I think it was about $200. I felt very humbled and privileged. I don't think too many whitefellas would have had such an experience. Little did we know back then of the importance of our relationship and what lay ahead.'

Helen Dunn of Ceduna, who knew her well for over 20 years, said, 'Although life was hard for Yvonne, she never stopped giving to others.'

Chapter Twelve

The lost is found

Yvonne and David's first baby was more fortunate than most Aboriginal children taken from their families. Because of government policy, most were put in children's homes or fostered out to whitefella parents. But their baby was adopted by a family who treated him as their own and honoured the name given him by his birth parents – Michael. Anita and Don Aspinall, who already had two sons, wanted to give another child, an Aboriginal child, a good start in life.

They went to a home in Adelaide where children were sent for adoption. Here they were shown children in the

DETAIL FROM 'COMING HOME TO FAMILY' | ARTWORK BY YVONNE EDWARDS, PHOTO BY PAM DIMENT, COURTESY OF TJUTJUNA ARTS & CULTURE CENTRE 'unadoptable' ward and encouraged, even pressured to take a whitefella boy. But on seeing six-week-old Michael, they knew at once that he was the child they wanted for their third son. When he smiled at them, staff were amazed. It was his first smile. It seemed as if he also knew.

He was wearing the little woollen jacket Yvonne had knitted for him and Anita asked for it. But the nurse said that it was needed for another child, as they were short of clothing. So Michael was not allowed to keep the warmth of his mother's love. And the Aspinalls were told that his mother had wanted to give him up. She had signed the papers.

When Michael was two years old, Anita met a Lutheran pastor at a conference and asked him if he would pass on a letter she wrote to tell Michael's mother that her son was doing well.

But Yvonne never received that letter.

Young Michael had a very happy childhood growing up with his three adoptive brothers, two older, one younger, receiving a good education, going on holidays, skiing, swimming, even travelling overseas when his adoptive father, an academic, took study leave, and then living for two years in Indonesia, when Don Aspinall,

MICHAEL ASPINALL (LEFT) AT HEATHFIELD PRIMARY SCHOOL, AND (RIGHT) AT HEATHFIELD HIGH SCHOOL | PHOTOS COURTESY OF ANITA ASPINALL

an agricultural scientist, served as a professor at an Indonesian university.

Michael was a happy, bright, intelligent child. He loved the only family he knew. And they all loved him. With pride Anita and Don watched as he developed into a fine young musician, learning the guitar, writing his own songs and leading his own band.

But when he became a teenager he began to question who he really was. Having never been given the little jacket his mother had knitted with such hope and love for him, he did not believe that his birth mother had loved him and still loved him. He did not know that she had been tricked into signing adoption papers. He did not know that his birth father was now an important man in his own community. He did not know that his A<u>n</u>angu parents had never stopped hoping to find him. Every year Anita told him that she knew who his parents were. Every year she asked if he wanted to contact them. But he always said no.

Then at last, in 1985, Yvonne and David found him. An Aboriginal man in a government department heard their story. Realising their sorrow, he talked to a journalist who told their story in the Adelaide *Advertiser*. And the very next day the phone at Yalata rang.

'We have your son Michael,' the whitefella voice said to Yvonne and David. 'He wants to come and meet you.'

So after 20 years of wondering, hoping, praying, longing to see their firstborn son, Yvonne and David waited while he drove the 1000 kilometres from Adelaide. They could scarcely sleep. They could scarcely eat or drink. How they longed to see him… Would he look like his father? Would he have his mother's eyes? Would he be tall like his father? Or short like his mother? Had he ever heard his mother tongue spoken? Would he know a word of it?

'COMING HOME TO FAMILY': THE TRACKS LEADING TO THE CENTRE SHOW THE CHILDREN, WHO HAVE BEEN TAKEN AWAY, COMING HOME. THE CENTRE OF THE PAINTING SHOWS THE COMMUNITY COMING TOGETHER, WHERE THE CHILDREN FIND THEIR FAMILIES. | ARTWORK BY YVONNE EDWARDS, PHOTO BY PAM DIMENT, COURTESY OF TJUTJUNA ARTS & CULTURE CENTRE

MICHAEL, 1984 | PHOTO COURTESY OF ANITA ASPINALL

David was nervous. Yvonne was scared. What would this son grown up by whitefellas think of them? What would he say? What would they say? What would they do? What would he do? As they waited, Yvonne prayed to her friend Jesus, remembering the story the missionaries had told about the son who had left home and at last returned to his father.

But her son had not left his home. He had been taken.

She remembered another story told by the missionaries about a woman who had lost one of her gold coins. She still had the others, but she searched and searched until she found the missing one. And when at last she did, she called her neighbours together to celebrate with her. It would be like that when Michael came home to his own people, home to his own family and community.

It was a day like no other when Michael arrived at last at Yalata to be welcomed by his mother and his father, his brothers and his sister, his aunts, his uncles, his cousins, the elders who knew his story and the whole community, rejoicing in the return of their own. Yvonne felt her heart would burst with happiness as she wept tears of joy.

Yvonne and David were proud of their firstborn son who had grown into a fine young man in this caring whitefella family – this family who would become their family too. And Michael was amazed and moved to be accepted and enfolded in this caring community.

Chapter Thirteen

The happiest years – Michael

At last Yvonne's heart was at peace. When Michael had told Yvonne and David that he wanted to come to Yalata to meet all his A<u>n</u>angu family and learn about his people's history, she knew again that her prayers over 20 years had been answered. Michael would always be deeply grateful for the love, nurture and opportunities his adoptive family had given him. But now it was time to learn about the people from whom the Welfare had taken him, the people whose history went back over 40 000 years. So he

DETAIL FROM 'GATHERING' | ARTWORK BY YVONNE EDWARDS, COURTESY OF TULLAWON HEALTH SERVICE, YALATA, PHOTO BY JESSIE BOYLAN made the long drive of 1000 kilometres from Adelaide, and as he passed each mile post he was wondering what was awaiting him at journey's end. A new beginning?

Michael was welcomed into the community with open arms. He was thrilled and in turn he opened his mind and heart to these Anangu, these aunts and uncles and cousins to whom he was inextricably linked. Michael was proud to see how Yvonne and David contributed to the community and the respect in which they were held. And to find himself with six more brothers and a sister all younger than he was, was a new experience, having been the second youngest in his adoptive family. Now he was the oldest in his Anangu family. But he had much to learn from his younger Anangu siblings and his birth parents. They took him camping, going for bush tucker, learning bush skills, learning from the night skies, learning language, learning stories, learning, always learning. So much to learn. So many years to catch up. But Michael was a good student. And he learned well.

As he observed Yvonne's skill with brush and canvas, Michael discovered the joys of expressing himself through painting. But while Yvonne's paintings celebrated sinuous and curving shapes, those Michael did at Yalata showed the influence of angles. Later his work would be seen by a visiting US academic, who took 20 of his paintings back to the University of Virginia Kluge-Rule Aboriginal Art Collection, where 12 were reproduced in a calendar. Other paintings went to Switzerland and to the Burrinja Cultural Centre at Upwey in Victoria's Dandenong Ranges.

Michael's adoptive brother, Richard, also wanted to find out about the people from whom Michael had been taken. He came for a visit and stayed for five and a half years. A natural organiser, he soon found ways of helping in administration, and was chosen for the role of co-ordinator of the Community Council, earned gratitude and respect for his contribution to community affairs. Anita also made the journey to Yalata to experience for herself something of the life of Michael's people. Michael did not settle permanently at Yalata. Nor did Richard. But back in Adelaide Michael pursued a career as an artist, while Richard, who had forged a special link with the Anangu, continued to work with Aboriginal organisations, in various parts of Australia, currently Western Australia.

For Yvonne and David it was a source of deep gladness. The lost was found, the link was restored. Their family was whole at last. And now they had a second

family where they were included, respected and welcomed. David spent one Easter with the Aspinalls. Yvonne came later with her youngest children.

> The lost was found, the link was restored. Their family was whole at last.

Yvonne's heart was flooded with happiness.

But another shadow was already looming.

Whitefella veterans who had been at Emu Field and Maralinga during the 1953 to 1963 nuclear tests had long campaigned for a Royal Commission into the British program and its effects, and finally in 1984 the Royal Commission into British Nuclear Tests in Australia was set up. A number of senior Pitjantjatjara men and women gave evidence, including Anangu Alice Cox, Rene Sandimar, the late Mabel Queama and Edie Milpuddie.

But David and Yvonne Edwards did not. They did not yet know how the black shadow of Maralinga's mushroom clouds was steadily moving towards them, to engulf them, their children and their grandchildren.

'TRACKS' BY MICHAEL ASPINALL, 1999 | YARRA RANGES COUNCIL, McLEOD GIFT COLLECTION, COURTESY OF BURRINJA CULTURAL CENTRE

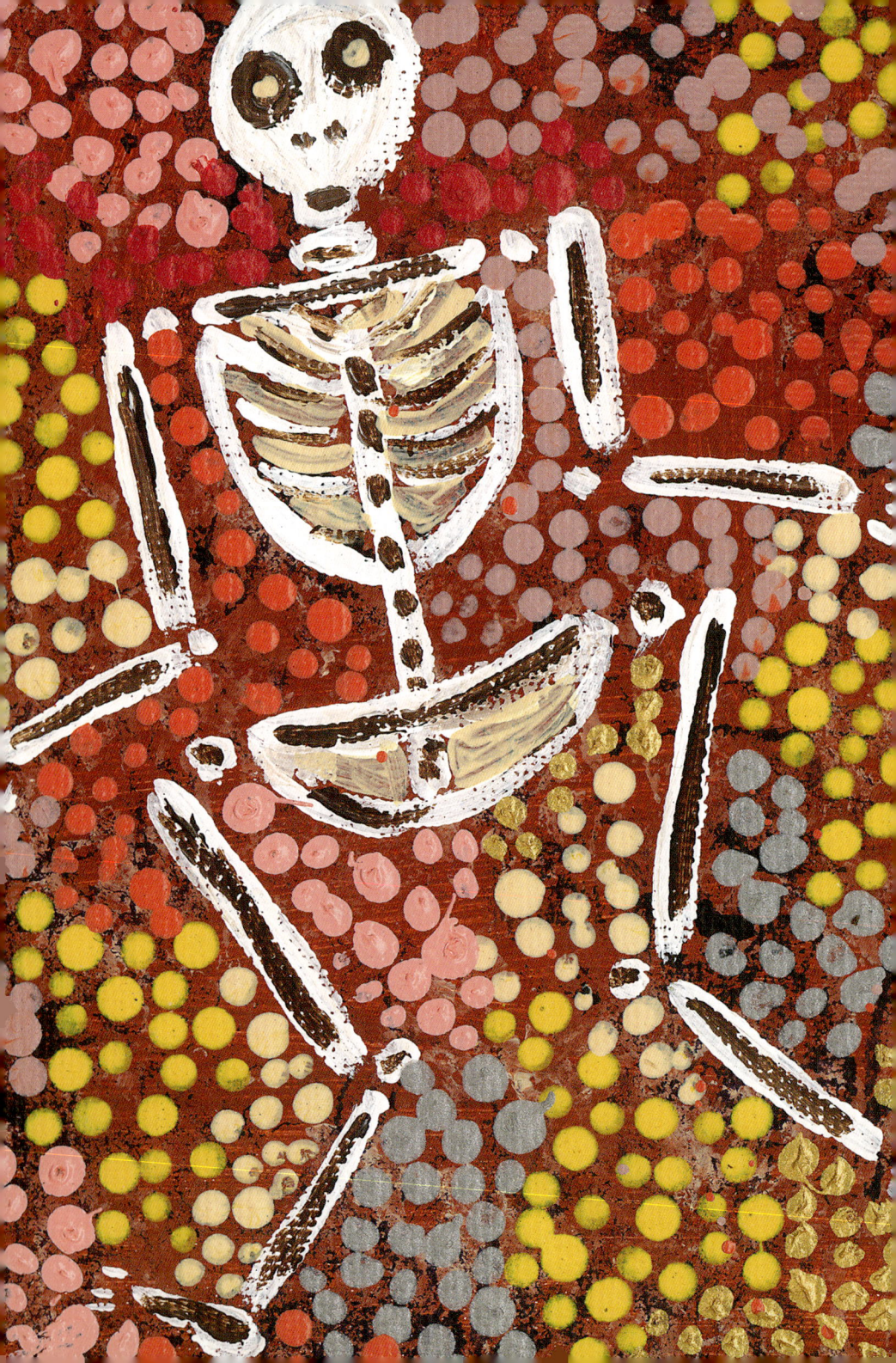

Chapter Fourteen

Cancer and the cemetery

Grief took its toll on the older people removed from their homelands. As did the effects of the British nuclear tests from 1953 to 1963. So one of the first permanent areas which had to be established at Yalata was the cemetery. Several kilometres from what was to become the centre of the settlement, earthen mounds, some marked by hand-fashioned wooden crosses, began to rise among the humps of silver saltbush, as Anangu young and old were laid to rest in foreign soil. And sorry camps and sorry

DETAIL FROM 'MARALINGA [I]' | ARTWORK BY YVONNE EDWARDS

YALATA CEMETERY, 2014 | PHOTO BY JESSIE BOYLAN

business disrupted whitefella calendars and schedules, as the community mourned stillborn infants, a child with a brain tumour, and respected elders who took with them knowledge of country they had been unable to pass on to the next generation.

In 1991 and 1992 a delegation of A<u>n</u>angu senior men went to Britain to try to obtain compensation for the damage caused by the British nuclear tests. David Edwards was not a member of the delegation, but like others he often spoke about the hazards of the 'clean-up' and the lack of compensation, declaring that the government of the day put little value on the life of an Aboriginal worker. Finally a settlement was reached and eventually in 1995 the British government paid money for clean-up and for compensation into a trust fund for the benefit of the communities.

But no amount of money could ever make up for the irreversible damage to A<u>n</u>angu health and heritage – to the ground on which A<u>n</u>angu had walked for countless generations, the ground on which they sat, cooked, ate, slept, made love, gave birth. The ground on which they celebrated age-old ceremonies and rituals. The land on which they hunted game and gathered fruit, roots and seeds. The land which guarded life-giving water in secret soaks and rockholes. The land which gave them life. The land they venerated. The land they loved with every fibre of their beings. The land, their mother.

When in 2003 David was diagnosed with lung cancer, Yvonne was devastated. She thought back in grief and anger to the long days and nights at Maralinga, when David had been engaged in the so-called clean-up. Driving the front-end loader moving contaminated soil and drums of poison. Not given the protective clothing with which whitefellas were issued. Exposed to the radioactive dust. Inhaling the deadly poison. Yvonne took some comfort, even pride, that the Queen herself had been told David's story. But no royal decree could banish cancer.

> No amount of money could ever make up for the irreversible damage to Anangu health and heritage.

And no amount of British money could change the situation David and Yvonne now faced.

Yvonne immediately made the courageous decision to move to Adelaide to be close to David while he underwent treatment. To live in the city was a huge

YVONNE C. 2006–8

challenge. She had already proved that she could adapt to new places and conditions. From Ooldea to Monburu to Tjinnalumba to Fowlers Bay to Yalata and travelling with David and their children for work all over Eyre Peninsula. And to Maralinga.

But Adelaide was so different from anywhere she had ever lived before. Roads in all directions, traffic lights, trams, trains, cars, buses, bicycles, noise, street lights, office towers storey upon storey upon storey, skyscrapers, shops, supermarkets, pubs, people. People everywhere and scarcely a dark face or a smile among them. She shrank from using public transport. But taking taxis was so expensive. And taxi drivers sometimes took her to a wrong address, then charged more to go to the address she had given. So she often had to wait until a family member could drive her where she needed to go.

And houses. Hundreds upon hundreds of houses. Thousands of houses. Houses jammed together, crammed together. Blocks of flats. Blocks of units. Fences, fences, fences, iron, brick, wood, wire. Fences and gates. Closed gates. Closed doors. Closed faces of people who knew nothing about A<u>n</u>angu and all they had suffered.

And the hospital. The huge hospital. Stairs, lifts, corridors, wards, whitefella nurses. Not good memories for Yvonne who had never forgotten how Michael was taken from her. But faithfully she went to be with David. David who was dying.

There were a few familiar faces. Other A<u>n</u>angu, afflicted with kidney disorders, had already been forced to make the move to Adelaide for access to dialysis not available then within reach of Yalata. A Lutheran pastor too, who had a special ministry to A<u>n</u>angu. And a Josephite sister who had worked at Yalata. Plus two teachers who had been at Yalata A<u>n</u>angu School when she had worked there as an assistant.

Determined as always to make the best of a bad situation, Yvonne began building a new life. Some neighbours were racist, some on alcohol or drugs were scary, even invasive, but one or two were helpful. She found unexpected pleasure in the opportunity to have a garden. And she welcomed family and friends from Yalata who came to stay for medical appointments or the football. When she could not meet the phone or food bills, she approached her teacher friends for a loan, which she always paid back on the morning she received her next pension payment. Or she painted a picture to sell. But one dealer only paid in cigarettes. One packet for a painting. So she might try her luck at the poker machines.

Despite the comforting support of frequent visits from Yvonne, as well as visits from family, David Edwards lost his fight against cancer. Nine days after Yvonne's 54th birthday, he died on 21 September 2004. After a long and happy marriage of 38 years, Yvonne could not contemplate having him buried in Adelaide so far from where he had spent his life. So he was returned to be laid to rest where he had spent so many years serving his people, trying to salvage lives and build a positive community at Yalata.

ALONG THE TRACK TO THE CEMETERY AT YALATA, 2014 | PHOTO BY JESSIE BOYLAN

At the sorry camp when it began to rain, Yvonne refused to move to shelter. She continued to sit under a tree, saying to her sister and friend Wanda Miller, 'The rain drops are tears falling from heaven.'

It was to be the first of three drives Yvonne was to make, following the hearse of a close member of her family over the dusty, stony track to the cemetery. It was growing steadily year by year among saltbush and twisted eucalypts tasselled with bark, whose leafy canopies looked like downturned saucers.

Yvonne and David's daughter Judy remembered, 'Before my father passed away when he was sick we used to stay as a family at the house at Mansfield Park. He had cancer, going for treatment every couple of days. We was here as family. I stayed couple of weeks, go home [to Amata], then come back.

'When he passed away in Royal Adelaide Hospital we was all there. Family came down on bus – all there. That day my family seen him and wanted to be with him. My mother wanted me to go outside, but I wanted to stay – be with him. First time for me – seeing someone pass away. Seeing my father pass away. Really hard. I was there when he did his last breath and finish. Only me. I was thinking and I saw an angel – rising up, flying up to heaven. I saw the angel who took my father to heaven. But I didn't tell my family, had it in my heart. I was sad but I was happy.

'That night he came back. He was shining and said to my mother, "I got no pain now. I went to a better place. I want you and Josie to look after my kids." Josie was a good auntie. Josie didn't see him, only my mother.'

Yvonne's tribute to her husband, 'I See You', in the traditional Yalata funeral booklet, said,

> I see you exhausted.
> I see you suffering.
> How tired you are.
> Illnesses has taken their toll.
> The pain you endure every day.
>
> I see you
> You are so courageous through your struggles,
> Every day you smile, you laugh, you go on,
> No matter how you feel.
>
> I see you
> I wonder why you have to be so ill
> I ask every day, why you, why us?

But you live your life to the full
You don't ask, you just accept.

Still grieving in 2009, Yvonne wondered, 'He had cancer all over his lungs. He's gone now. Why didn't they let my husband wear the protective clothing? That dust was no good. I always think about it. My husband used to ask for compensation. But they always said NO. We got nothing.'

Yvonne's grief and anger were to grow over the next eight years as Maralinga cast its ever-lengthening shadow over her family. But her next drive to a funeral was to be very different. A long way from Yalata, among towering gum trees back in the lush green Adelaide Hills.

Chapter Fifteen

Another loss

In 2006 Yvonne found a new outlet for her creativity, working with a group of senior ladies telling and illustrating the story of their displacement by British atomic testing in the book *Maralinga: The Anangu Story*. She was the best informant with very clear memories, reliving events as she told them, her voice rising and dropping, almost trance-like as she spoke of stories and customs handed down from time immemorial. She was also the best artist, often helping those less skilled to complete their paintings. Sitting on the floor to work or, better still, outside on the ground by a little fire, using a rich range

DETAIL FROM 'SEVEN SISTERS' | ARTWORK BY YVONNE EDWARDS, PHOTO BY JESSIE BOYLAN, COURTESY OF TULLAWON HEALTH SERVICE, YALATA of colours she skilfully created a series of images based on life as she and her people knew it – bush tucker, traditional implements, *Waṉampi*, the Rainbow Serpent, the effects of grog and the devastation caused by the nuclear explosions.

MARALINGA: THE AṈANGU STORY WORKSHOP, 2008 | PHOTOS BY GEOFF WILLSMORE

Using a rich range of colours Yvonne skilfully created a series of images based on life as she and her people knew it.

In 2007, the second workshop for the book was almost brought to a halt when her brother Colin, husband of Yalata Community Chairperson Mima Smart, was admitted to the Royal Adelaide Hospital, seriously ill. It was another anxious time of fervent prayer by Yvonne. Colin made a recovery and work on the book resumed. Deeply concerned about making a better future for their children and grandchildren, Mima, Yvonne and the other women involved in the book agreed that all royalties earned should go to a fund to provide educational opportunities for the young people of Yalata and Oak Valley.

Then in 2008 Yvonne suffered another devastating loss. Michael was severely injured in a road accident. Yet again she became a frequent visitor to the dauntingly big hospital in Adelaide, sitting for hours at his bedside in the intensive care unit, praying, always praying, hoping against hope for him to recover sufficiently to undergo surgery. But after six agonising weeks the decision was made to switch off the life support. Both families were desolate and came together to organise his funeral.

The little Anglican church at Longwood in the Adelaide Hills, where Michael had been baptised, had been destroyed in the 1981 bushfires. So the service was held at Scotts Creek where Michael had grown up, and the Memorial Hall was filled to overflowing, as Anangu family and friends had made the long journey from Yalata to pay their last respects, to support Yvonne in her sorrow and to farewell her firstborn son. Slowly the funeral procession wound its way along the narrow dirt road beneath towering gum trees to the peaceful little cemetery where Michael was laid to rest. So far from the place of his birth, but as Michael had wished, close to the grave of his adoptive father, Don Aspinall, who had given him so much.

Yvonne took comfort that Michael's grave was facing west into the setting sun – towards Yalata.

Chapter Sixteen

Maralinga's long shadow

First it was David dying in 2004. Then in 2008 the Edwards family suffered two more blows. Michael died just seven days after Yvonne's 58th birthday. Yvonne and David's youngest son, Aaron, and his wife, Kristy, were devastated when their first child, Dominic, was born in Port Augusta with a malfunctioning digestive system. He was immediately transferred to the Women and Children's Hospital in Adelaide, where he spent the

DETAIL FROM 'MARALINGA [I]': ELDER GRIEVING AT THE DESECRATION OF COUNTRY AND THE DEATHS OF ITS PEOPLE AND ANIMALS | ARTWORK BY YVONNE EDWARDS

next 13 months being fed by tube, then three more years in and out of hospital for treatment.

Yvonne thought back to the time she and David had spent at Maralinga. So Maralinga was now leaving its mark on their grandchild. Kristy and Aaron also reflected on Dominic's condition and what had caused it. Kristy had grown up in Kalgoorlie, almost 1000 kilometres from Maralinga, and her parents had never worked at Maralinga. She had five sisters, all married, who still lived in Kalgoorlie and who, between them, had 12 children. Twelve normal healthy children. But Aaron's father had driven a front-end loader through the contaminated dirt at Maralinga. Without protective clothing. And he had paid the ultimate price. Now Maralinga's shadow had fallen on his grandson.

Yvonne was thankful she was living in Adelaide so that the young parents could stay with her, as they went every day to visit their baby, the little grandson she loved. After he was discharged they still lived with her as they had to continue the tube feeding for three more years, with regular check-ups at the hospital. She watched his progress with pride. Then at the age of five he was diagnosed as autistic.

After long troubles at her duplex with drug addict

neighbours, Yvonne was very happy when the Housing Trust found her a new place in another suburb – a freestanding brick house in its own grounds in a quiet street with neat houses and tended gardens, and a sports ground at the end where her grandchildren could kick balls and run on grass when they came from Yalata. Her house had a front lawn too and there were shrubs in the neighbours' yards, hibiscus with red flowers which reminded her of the *malukuru* that she loved.

At the back there was a mandarin tree and a rainwater tank, and best of all, a wide verandah where she loved to paint, sitting in the sun with family and friends around her. There was also a big iron garage which became her workshop for making artefacts. With the door wide open she could see anyone coming in from the street, while a gate to the big backyard meant her precious little grandson, now toddling, could not stray into the driveway and out onto the road.

Yvonne was happy. 'There's peace, peace. Quiet. Safe. I can paint here.'

She wanted to paint. And she needed to paint because her pension was not enough to pay for the petrol, the food, the phone bills. Everyone from Yalata loved to come and stay for the football or just for a visit. Family and friends knew they were always welcome at Yvonne's and it was often full house. For the first time in a long while Yvonne felt happy and settled. But sometimes there was not enough money to pay for the canvas and paint.

Then a phone call to whitefella friends for a loan, which was always paid back promptly on the morning of pension day. Yvonne was no bludger. A few days later another phone call to a whitefella friend. 'I got a painting. You know someone who buy it?'

Yvonne was happy. But not for long.

In 2009 she and her family had to suffer another ordeal. This time it was her son Patrick who was diagnosed with cancer. In and out of hospital. From home to hospital. From Yalata to Port Augusta Hospital. From Port Augusta home to Yalata. Yvonne catching the bus to Port Augusta. The bus back to Adelaide. Then to Port Augusta again. And again. Yvonne prayed. She had already lost her husband to cancer. She had lost her firstborn son. Surely not another death? Patrick's daughter growing up without her father? No wonder Yvonne painted a grieving elder in a mushroom cloud.

In April 2009, *Maralinga: The Anangu Story* was published and over 400 people, Aboriginal and whitefella,

LEFT TO RIGHT: MIMA SMART, YVONNE AND JOSIE MACARTHUR READING AN ADVANCE COPY OF *MARALINGA: THE ANANGU STORY*, FEBRUARY 2009 | PHOTO BY CHRISTOBEL MATTINGLEY

crowded into the Tandanya National Aboriginal Cultural Institute in Adelaide for its launch by survivor and anti-nuclear campaigner Yami Lester. Busloads of Anangu, including venerated elder Alice Cox, proud and regal in her wheelchair, came from Yalata and Oak Valley for the occasion. Yvonne and the other senior ladies were interviewed by ABC television and their paintings were on exhibition.

Artist and former ABC host Charles Southwood, who spoke at the launch about the paintings, said: 'The reality of Maralinga is raw and red and dreadful. It is a reality lodged like a barb in the flesh of the people who one way or another had to live through that time. And it's that very flesh, the very hands of these people, which took up brush and paint and took the risk of laying out the images of horror and beauty which inform us tonight. Inform but do so much more beside. This isn't even mere "art". It's guts. This is the direct imprint of lives actually lived.'

Later in 2009, ABC's *Message Stick* made two documentaries based on *Maralinga: The A̱nangu Story* and they were among the most watched of all its year's programs, gaining some of the biggest audiences. Several of Yvonne's paintings featured in the films and she spoke passionately for her people and the terrible injustice they had suffered. 'Nobody would like to live there now. The damage that's been done – you can't fix that. It's not good to live there any more.'

Maralinga: The A̱nangu Story quickly went into two reprints and a paperback edition, also reprinted, and was an Honour Book in the Children's Book Council of Australia's 2010 awards, as well as being shortlisted for several other awards. Its publication brought long overdue attention to the suffering the A̱nangu had endured because of the British nuclear tests.

In 2010, the 56 paintings made for the book were included as part of the International Women's Day exhibition in St Peter's Cathedral, Adelaide. Laid out on the steps leading to the sanctuary, they made a dramatic statement, and Yvonne's image of the Seven Sisters, painted for the exhibition, quickly sold. Then, as part of

THE PAINTINGS AT THE INTERNATIONAL WOMEN'S DAY EXHIBITION IN ST PETER'S CATHEDRAL, ADELAIDE, 2010 | PHOTO BY CHRISTOBEL MATTINGLEY

the 2010 Gladys Elphick Awards ceremony in Adelaide, an award to 'The Twelve Strong Anangu Women' involved in the creation of the book was presented to them by the Governor of South Australia. The book's paintings later toured regional South Australian art galleries for two years, and were also displayed at the University of Sydney Conservatorium of Music.

When asked to do a painting for St David's Anglican Church at Burnside, South Australia, for its annual reconciliation service, Yvonne agreed at once, saying, 'I know what I'll do.' Five days later she phoned to say, 'Painting ready.' She had done a dramatic depiction of the crucifixion scene, with three empty crosses and mourners shown by typical symbols at the base. The painting, which hangs permanently in the church, has been used as a cover image for the Adelaide *Church Guardian* and another Anglicare publication.

Meantime on 18 December 2009, after much negotiation between the Commonwealth and South Australian governments, the last portion of the lands forcibly taken over for the British atomic tests, the so-called Section 400, was officially handed back to Maralinga Tjarutja, the organisation representing the Anangu people. Anangu in their hundreds came by bus,

'CRUCIFIXION', COMMISSIONED BY CHRISTOBEL MATTINGLEY FOR ST DAVID'S ANGLICAN CHURCH AT BURNSIDE, SOUTH AUSTRALIA | ARTWORK BY YVONNE EDWARDS, PHOTO BY ERICA WAGNER

car, truck, 4WD. Through the big gates, past the high chain wire fences which had shut them out for over 57 years. Back on to their own land. Back on to the land from which they had been so cruelly evicted in 1952. A few even came by plane, stepping out onto the vast concrete runway, in its time the longest and strongest in the southern hemisphere. The runway built for the planes bringing the British scientists to experiment with poison on Anangu lands. The runway from which the bombers had taken off. The bombers from which those lethal nuclear weapons had been dropped.

Many Anangu camped overnight on their mother earth. Their mother earth which was still overlaid with the grids of the whitefella streets with their English names. The earth on which the hospital, the water tower, the flagpole and one of the accommodation and recreation blocks still stood. The earth which still radiated heat. Anangu Andrea Richards and her family, from Ceduna, woke in their tents during the night. Andrea said, 'It was weird. We could feel heat under our pillows, under our mattresses. It was eerie. We freaked out. My parents and sister moved into the bus to sleep.'

Proud and jubilant in their celebratory orange T-shirts, Anangu wandered over their desecrated country, sat on the desecrated ground. Sharing memories. Grieving. Rejoicing.

Yvonne, in her orange T-shirt, a colour she loved, smiled to see her grandson, toddler Dominic, wandering over the grounds where she and David had walked 35 years ago. If only David could be here today. With their sons. With their daughter. If only he could be here in an

LEFT TO RIGHT: YVONNE, THOMAS SANDIMAR, AARON EDWARDS, KAYLENE SANDIMAR AND MARJORIE SANDIMAR AT THE HANDBACK OF SECTION 400 OF THE MARALINGA TJARUTJA LANDS, DECEMBER 2009 | PHOTO BY DR ROSEMARY BROOKS

orange T-shirt, celebrating too. If only those whitefellas had given him protective clothing, boots, gloves, hood, goggles and a mask like they had worn ...

Whitefella dignitaries arrived. The Governor of South Australia. Government ministers from Canberra and Adelaide. Everyone sat on white plastic chairs set out in rows – whitefellas to one side, A*n*angu to the other. Alice Cox was in her wheelchair, with Yvonne beside her. Whitefellas made speeches. In English of course. The Federal Minister for Aboriginal Affairs used many passages from *Maralinga: The A*n*angu Story*. And at last the Aboriginal flag was raised on the flagpole and the plaque, which had been set up the day before, was unveiled. Wind whispered in the eucalypts as the whitefellas expressed regret. Officially they handed back the last of the Maralinga land to its traditional custodians. To the A*n*angu.

To the A*n*angu who had cared for it respectfully and faithfully from time immemorial. To the A*n*angu who did not measure time in years, but in seasons, with the wind whispering in the eucalypts, and the bees humming in its blossoms. With the *ma*l*uku*r*u* carpeting the earth in

THE PLAQUE COMMEMORATING THE OFFICIAL HANDBACK OF SECTION 400 TO THE MARALINGA TJARUTJA | PHOTO BY DR ROSEMARY BROOKS

Government of South Australia

SECTION 400

His Excellency Rear Admiral Kevin Scarce AC CSC RANR
Governor of South Australia

unveiled this plaque on
18 December 2009
to commemorate the handback to
Maralinga Tjarutja of Section 400,
which includes the former British Nuclear Test and
Minor Trial sites and the Maralinga Village.

MARALINGA TJARUTJA

The Tommy Queama, Jack Baker, Dr Archie Barton AM Memorial

18th December 2009

In recognition of community members that made this day possible

† Nellie Queama
† James Peters
† Rene Sandimar
† Steven York
† Jimmy Young
† Jack May
† Herbert Queama
† Joe Smart
† Cyril Cook

Hughie Windlass
† Peter Pepper
† Mervyn Day
† Jeffrey Queama
Richard LeBois
Barka Bryant
Braddon Queama
Warren Bryant
† Jimmy Pinky

† Alex Long
† May Baker
† Robert Baker
† Donald Baker
† Bobby Jones
† May Day
† Edie Milpuddie
† Paul Sandimar

scarlet. With the *nganamara* (mallee fowl) building their nesting mounds. With the *malu* (red kangaroos) and *kalaya* (emus) for hunting, the *maku* for digging, and the *wayanu tjuta* (quandongs) and *ili* (wild figs) for gathering.

But one section of the Maralinga lands, damaged beyond repair, remains a NO-GO ZONE. *NGURA WIYA*. Forever.

Whitefella dignitaries had lunch in a special marquee at round tables with white cloths and bowls of plastic flowers. Anangu ate outside. There was plenty of food for everyone. The planes took off for Canberra and Adelaide. The cars, the buses, the trucks, the 4WDs began to leave. Soon it was a ghost town again. Haunted forever by the inhumanities of the past. And out beyond the airstrip, out beyond the undulating waves of mallee and mulga, stretched the NGURA WIYA. Scorched earth. Bare. Burned. Barren. A No-Go Zone. Forever. Poisoned by plutonium.*

> NGURA WIYA. Scorched earth. Bare. Burned. Barren. A No-Go Zone. Forever.

---

* On 5 November 2014 the federal government returned the final 1782 square kilometre section, which had been retained by the Department of Defence as part of the Woomera Prohibited Area.

Less than four months after the handover, on 12 April 2010, Yvonne and David's second son, Patrick, died. Cancer took his life, as it had his father's.

Then, in 2011, Maralinga claimed another victim from the Edwards family. David and Yvonne's third son, Jamie. When he was diagnosed with cancer, he kept the news from his mother for as long as possible. But as his condition worsened and he grew weaker, she had to be told. Family and friends rallied round his bedside, yarning, joking, singing, praying. Jamie waited until Aaron arrived from Adelaide and the family circle was complete. Then he quietly slipped away.

After painting and sharing information for *Maralinga: The Anangu Story*, Yvonne wanted to tell her own story in her own book. She knew that people beyond Yalata needed to know what Maralinga had meant to her family. Needed to know what atomic weapons did to innocent people. But first with Michael's death, then Patrick's and now Jamie's, she felt unable to begin. Talking about the past was too painful. And she did not have the spirit to paint the story so close to her heart. For four long years as she faced one bereavement after another, her story remained untold.

Chapter Seventeen

Too young to die

By now Yvonne had diabetes and other health problems. Night after night she prayed. Prayed to be allowed to live to see her precious grandchildren grow up. Prayed for their safety and the safety of all her family. Then one night she knew her prayer had been answered. It was not the answer she had asked for. But an answer even more profound. No longer was she afraid of dying. She told her God, 'I am ready to die. I am ready to come whenever you want me. I want to be with my husband and my sons who are with you.'

And she told a friend, 'I expect to die soon.'

DETAIL FROM 'CRUCIFIXION' | ARTWORK BY YVONNE EDWARDS, PHOTO BY ERICA WAGNER

She had confidence in a doctor at Port Augusta who knew and understood A<u>n</u>angu. She preferred to go to him for help when she needed it, making the journey from Adelaide or from Yalata. But early in 2012, after moving into her next home, in the middle of a row of brand new closely packed houses, she was happy to be in Adelaide, and started yet again to put down roots by beginning to plant a garden. Down the narrow strip between her house and the next she put in cuttings of hardy succulents from friends, and planned to add fruit trees at the back when the weather became cooler and the autumn rain came. Meantime she filled the window ledges of the family room and kitchen overlooking the bare yard with bright bunches of plastic flowers.

And she knew that she was ready now to begin to tell her story. Early in March 2012 she phoned the friend she had asked to help her. 'When are we going to start my book?'

But Yvonne never planted the fruit trees. She never began work on the book her heart was set on creating. She never saw her newest grandchild, Aaron and Kristy's baby daughter, Taylor Noreen, named Noreen for Yvonne's sister who had died so young of cancer. When Kristy went into labour, she had been airlifted from

Kalgoorlie, where she was staying with her family, to Perth. There Taylor was born three months premature with problems. After three months in a Perth hospital, she was transferred for further treatment to the Women and Children's Hospital in Adelaide, where her brother Dominic had spent 13 months. Yvonne was eagerly awaiting the family's arrival. It was late at night, and knowing how tired from travel they would be and as she had a slight cold, Yvonne decided to defer her visit.

But next morning, 15 March 2012, Yvonne collapsed. She was rushed to the Queen Elizabeth Hospital, where she remained on life support for 22 days. Family and friends gathered anxiously in the waiting room outside the intensive care unit and were permitted to come to her bedside one at a time. A copy of *Maralinga: The Anangu Story* was brought for the staff to see what an important person they were caring for. Baby Taylor was brought and laid on her breast. But Yvonne's eyes did not open to see her.

Yvonne did not respond to treatment. She was moved to a private room and two days later, on 7 April 2012, when family had momentarily left, she died with three friends at her bedside. The small strong brown hands, which had dug for *maku* (witchetty grubs) and *watu* (wombats), cooked kangaroo tails and *kalta* (sleepy lizards) in camp fires, comforted babies, washed and worked tirelessly for others, gathered plants and created bush medicine, carved quandong and *gudia*, wielded paintbrushes with such skill, lay still on the white sheets. The voice which had told stories and taught children, sung praises and prayed, was silent.

> The voice which had told stories and taught children, sung praises and prayed, was silent.

Yvonne was 61. David was 64 when he died. Michael was 43. Patrick was 43. Jamie was 42. Yvonne's lament, 'We've got no old people now,' was being fulfilled. But the class action against the British government for compensation by veterans and Anangu affected by British nuclear tests, failed.[*]

There was a two-minute silence in Yvonne's honour at half-time in the APY Lands/Maralinga Tjarutja Football Carnival, which she had always supported with energy and passion, and a sorry camp, where others now

---

[*] Veterans and Anangu, including Yvonne, joined in 2011 to lodge a class action against the British Government. It was dismissed on the grounds of being beyond the time limit.

took up the tasks she had performed so willingly for so long. Then more people began arriving, travelling great distances to attend the funeral at Yalata. On the bright morning of Friday 27 April, cars were still arriving and people were gathering in hushed grief. The Lutheran Church of the Good Shepherd, where Yvonne had always been a faithful worshipper, overflowed with members of Yvonne's family, friends and community, and an ever-growing crowd stood around outside, listening to the tributes to this remarkable woman whose life had blessed so many.

A hundred and more vehicles, cars, 4WDs, trucks, minibuses and people-movers, all filled to capacity, followed the hearse as it drove through the bush along the dusty, stony track to the cemetery. The cemetery which had become a focal point in the lives of Yalata people. A place to visit. With family. With friends. In the afternoons when the sun was slanting through the trees. A place to reflect. To remember. To share stories. To weep. Sometimes to laugh. Simple earthen mounds, graves of the old people, scattered through the bush. Unmarked but remembered. Graves of the next generations in row after row with headstones and wooden crosses. Tiny graves marked with white plaster angels. Bigger graves

bright with plastic flowers. Coming to the cemetery through the saltbush and the scrub where grey thrushes whistled, from the distance it looked like a carpet of wildflowers of every colour.

The dust rose up in clouds, swirling through the scrub where the eucalypts stood stark against the autumn sky. People left their vehicles and walked to the gate to join the crowd already gathered, wailing, weeping, clutching plastic flowers of every size, shape and colour, colours which had delighted the eyes of Yvonne, the artist. As she was laid to rest beside her husband and two sons, the mourners placed the flowers in a last rainbow tribute. Giving thanks for a life most graciously and gallantly lived.

Then each sprinkled a handful of earth. The pale earth so different from the red sand of Tjintjiwara's birthplace, the country from which she and her people had been so callously uprooted 60 years before.

THE LUTHERAN CHURCH OF THE GOOD SHEPHERD, WHERE YVONNE'S FUNERAL SERVICE WAS HELD | PHOTO BY JESSIE BOYLAN; **OVERLEAF:** *MALUKURU* (STURT'S DESERT PEA) | PHOTO BY KETURAH DE KLERK/PHOTOGRAPHY LIFE

Author's note

I first went to Yalata in Children's Book Week in 1981 and was delighted by the children's interest and responsiveness. A boy at the back of the room was quick to call out 'Eagle! Eagle!' as he saw the eagle brooch, carved from Scottish horn, on my jacket. Perhaps he was one of Yvonne's sons.

I returned to Yalata in 1998 and 1999, but did not meet Yvonne Edwards until 2006.

In 1984, with the 150th anniversary of European settlement of 'South Australia' to be celebrated in 1986,

DETAIL FROM '*MUNDA* (COUNTRY) WITH SPINIFEX (CENTRE) SURROUNDED BY DIFFERENT OCHRES' | ARTWORK BY YVONNE EDWARDS, PHOTO BY PAM DIMENT, COURTESY OF TJUTJUNA ARTS & CULTURE CENTRE

an Aboriginal committee appointed me to research, edit and produce a book telling the Aboriginal side of those 150 years. Also in 1984, the Royal Commission into British Nuclear Tests in South Australia was established. After many problems with the government, *Survival in Our Own Land: 'Aboriginal' Experiences in 'South Australia' since 1836* was published in 1988, with a chapter, 'Atom Bombs before Aborigines', about the effects of the British nuclear tests at Maralinga.

In 2001, when white Australia was celebrating 100 years of federation, Aboriginal peoples from across the continent gathered in the centre at Alice Springs to celebrate their survival at the magnificent Yeperenye Festival. One event was the launch by Allen & Unwin of the beautiful *Papunya School Book of Country and History*, and on seeing it I said to publisher Erica Wagner, 'I'd love to do a book like this with the Anangu people.' 'You're on,' was her immediate reply.

In 2006, teachers Geoff and Jan Willsmore, who remembered my visit to Yalata in 1981, introduced me to the chairperson of Yalata Council, Mima Smart. She saw the importance of such a book and assembled a group of eight senior Anangu women to work with me. They came for a meeting at our home with Erica to discuss the book. And that was how I came to know Yvonne Edwards.

Several months later we gathered for our first workshop about the book at Nunyara, Belair, in the Adelaide Hills. Yvonne was the best artist in the group and often helped others, as well as completing a number of beautiful works of her own. She also proved to be the best informant, with a strong sense of story. On the second day we took a picnic into the national park, and there, after lunch, amid the trees and the birds, away from the hostel buildings and the state-of-the-art recording apparatus on loan from the State Library of South Australia, Yvonne opened up. As we sat in the spring sunshine at a rough picnic table away from the others listening to the football on the car radio, I scribbled and scribbled in my notebook, while Yvonne told of the pain of her people caused by the 10 years of British atomic tests on traditional A<u>n</u>angu lands.

That night I went home and sat at my computer until the small hours setting down all that Yvonne had shared in her low, slow, husky voice, which rose from time to time in anguish and anger. I can still hear her voice as I write now.

After the second workshop, some of the women and their menfolk came to our home to complete unfinished paintings. They were delighted to spot a koala in one of the big gum trees nearby, and whenever they came again, they would always look for koalas. Yvonne loved our garden and wanted to make one of her own. She tried and enjoyed the tang of cumquats and the spicy heat of nasturtium leaves. She loved lavender and rosemary, which she used for making bush medicine, and the bright red feathery flowers of callistemon. She was happy relaxing with a cuppa tea in the sun on the terrace, listening to the lorikeets and chuckling over the comings and goings of the lively little skinks.

Mima and Yvonne also came with me to the Lutheran Archives in search of photos and great was the excitement when we found one of Yvonne's brother Colin as a boy, because Colin was now Mima's husband.

When the advance copy of *Maralinga: The A<u>n</u>angu Story* arrived, I took it to Yvonne, then living in a duplex with unfriendly neighbours. She sat holding the precious book with her sister-in-law Mima Smart and her sister Aboriginal way Josie MacArthur on either side, and I took photos as they turned each page. It was a unique event, never to be forgotten.

Yvonne had said that she wanted to tell her own story in her own book and had asked me to help. But before we could begin, another tragedy overtook her. She had already lost her husband David to cancer. Now she was to lose their firstborn son, Michael. For the second time. He had been taken from her soon after birth and it was twenty years before she and David found him. Now, after a road accident he was on life support awaiting surgery. But after six weeks he died.

Yvonne was devastated. 'I can't paint,' she told me. 'I can't do my story.'

'We'll do it when you're ready,' I said.

But later, just as Yvonne had begun to cope with her grief, another blow fell. Patrick, her second son, was diagnosed with cancer. We sat together at the Port Augusta Hospital where he was having treatment and where Yvonne was staying in the Stepdown Hostel, hoping for the cure that was not to be. I was on the way to Yalata and Oak Valley with an ABC film crew to make a documentary about the Maralinga nuclear tests and their effects on the Anangu. At the end of the film shoot we caught up with Yvonne again in Adelaide. It was hard to find a suitable place for sound recording her interview. After an hour's searching, it somehow seemed symbolic that she was filmed against a corrugated iron fence as she spoke strongly and powerfully about the devastation the tests had brought to her people and their country.

A year after Patrick's death, Yvonne's third son, Jamie, died of cancer. And as if that was not enough, her latest grandson, little Dominic, first child of her youngest son, Aaron, had been born with a stomach defect which would keep him in hospital for over a year, tube fed for four years. Yvonne's faith was sorely tested, but she never lost it.

CHRISTOBEL MATTINGLEY AND YVONNE EDWARD APPEARING ON THE ABC'S *MESSAGE STICK* DOCUMENTARY IN 2009 | PHOTOS BY DENNIS BRENNAN, COURTESY OF MESSAGE STICK

On 7 March 2012 she phoned me. 'Christobel, when are we going to start my book?'

'As soon as you like, Yvonne,' I replied.

But a week later, before we had begun, on 15 March, Yvonne collapsed. She remained on life support for 22 days and died two days later, on 7 April 2012.

Then her name could not be mentioned and I had to wait for two years before I could begin work on her book. Now I dedicate it to her, with love.

Christobel Mattingley, Stonyfell, South Australia, 2015

MARALINGA, 18 DECEMBER 2009

The day the desert oaks stopped sighing
the day the desert oaks stopped crying
the day the gum leaves hung serenely still
the perfect summer day

The day of healing of old hurts
the day of soothing of old pains
the day of new hopes
the day of new beginnings

The day the Anangu were given back
the last of their lands so cruelly usurped
for British nuclear testing in 1953
Section 400 Maralinga Tjarutja
where nine atomic bombs were exploded
where 700 'minor trials' released
deadly beryllium, deadly plutonium
poisoning their age-old heritage
the land their mother
their Stolen Mother
from whose breast they were torn in 1952.

Christobel Mattingley

NORTHERN

Amata

WESTERN
AUSTRALIA

Wallatinna

Emu Field (Emu Junction)

GREAT VICTORIA DESERT

Oak Valley

◀ Kalgoorlie

NULLARBOR PLAIN

Ooldea (Yuldi)

Maralinga

Middle Yard

Ooldea Tank (Monburu)

Nullarbor

Yalata

Tjinnalumba (Chinnalumba) Tank

Penor

Nundroo

Coorabie

Fowlers Bay

GREAT AUSTRALIAN BIGHT

⊢—⊣ 100 KM APPROX.

TERRITORY

SOUTH
AUSTRALIA

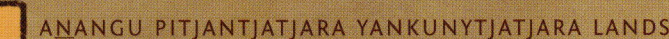 ANANGU PITJANTJATJARA YANKUNYTJATJARA LANDS
 MARALINGA TJARUTJA LANDS

Koonibba
Ceduna

● Port Augusta

● Port Lincoln

● Adelaide

Glossary

Pitjantjatjara is the language most widely spoken by the Western Desert peoples.

A<u>n</u>angu	people; name used by Aboriginal peoples of the Western Desert when referring to themselves
i<u>l</u>i	wild fig
inma	songs, ceremony, dances
gudia	Western myall
ka<u>l</u>aya	emu
kalta	sleepy lizard
kapa<u>l</u>i	grandmother
kapi	water
kata	head
kipa<u>r</u>a	bustard, bush turkey
kuka	meat
kuturu	stick used by senior women as a symbol of leadership
maku	witchetty grub
mulapa	true, real
ma<u>l</u>u	red kangaroo
ma<u>l</u>uku<u>r</u>u	Sturt's desert pea; literally kangaroo eye

mamu	evil spirit
maru	port, fortified wine, grog
mur̲untu	snake
ngan̲amara	mallee fowl
ngura wiya	no-go zone
palya	good
pan̲a	earth, land
piti	wooden bowl or dish
pun̲u	piece of wood, tree, bush
tjamu	grandfather, grandson
tjil̲pi	old, old man, elder
tjitji	child
Tjukur(pa)	the law and lore of the An̲angu, their stories, the Dreaming
tjuta	many, lots; used to indicate plural
tuuni	thunder
walypala	white man (from English 'whitefella')
Wan̲ampi	water snake that guards waterholes; Rainbow Serpent
wat̲u	wombat
wayan̲u	quandong
wira	wooden scoops or bowls, used for carrying food and water
wiya	no, nothing, none

Pronunciation: Curl your tongue back slightly to say the underlined consonants. 'Ng' at the beginning of words sounds like the end of 'sing'.

Acknowledgements

Many people have had a part in honouring Yvonne in this book and I am grateful to them all for their contributions.

I thank Yvonne's sons, Duane, Teddy, Terence and Aaron, and her daughter, Judy, for approving the draft of their mother's story, her brother Ronald Murka for his approval, her sister Wanda Miller for sharing precious memories, and Eileen Miller for arranging family conferencing with me, and for supplying Yvonne's, David's and Jamie's funeral booklets. I thank Yvonne's wider family and friends for the use of their heartfelt tributes in her funeral booklet.

I thank Erica Wagner for her belief in the importance of Yvonne's story, Sophie Splatt for her care in editing, Karin Riederer for her care in proofreading and providing contacts, and designer Ruth Grüner for this beautiful book.

I thank Professor Paul Brown for helping with expenses connected with research and airfares to and from Ceduna.

I thank Jessie Boylan, Keturah de Klerk, Pam Diment, Danielle Marwick, Dr Rosemary Brooks, Geoff and Jan Willsmore, Tom Stringer, Bill Dowling and Dennis Brennan for photography, and Fran Zilio at the SA Museum and Janette Lange at the SA Lutheran Archives for their help in finding archival photos. For making their paintings by Yvonne available to be used in this book I thank Dr Alan and Elizabeth Brissenden, Professor Anne Boyd, Bev Firth and Andrew Moore, Maureen and Rob Brooks, the Tullawon Health Service and Ceduna (Tjutjuna) Aboriginal Arts & Culture Centre.

I thank Michele Madigan, Pam Diment, Val Surch, Josie MacArthur, Marjorie Sandimar, Anita Aspinall, Richard Aspinall, Helen Dunn, Eve Dobbins, Grant Fiedler, Pastor Bryce Clark and Judy Clark, Pastor Dean Heyne, Clarrie Oster, Bob Sim, Charles Southwood, David and Ruth Craig, Linda Zerk, Dr Ashley Thomas, Rita Bryant, Margaret May,

Ashley Milroy, Andrea Richards, Matthew Kelly, Ineke Gilbert, Barbara Robinson-Tan and the Sisters of St Joseph, for sharing memories and information, and David, Rosemary and Stephen Mattingley, for their support and help in many ways, and St David's Anglican Church, Burnside, SA, Ildi Wetherell, Ray Booth, Bishop Chris McLeod, Chris Guille, Peter and Vicky Balabanski, Mark Waters, Jenny Francis, Bernie and Barbara Boxer, Maxine and Gordon Goulding, Rosanne Hawke, Russell Bryant and Rachel Kuchel for their help.

I thank Greg Franks for permission to be on community at various times, community members for making me welcome, and Bob Sim, Vivien Deed, Georgie Mudge and Steve Harrison for providing accommodation on my visits to Yalata and Oak Valley.

I thank Andrew Collett for facilitating my trip to Maralinga for the 2009 official handbook of Section 400 to the Anangu, and the ABC's *Message Stick* team, Pauline Clague, Dennis Brennan and Laura Howard – especially for their patience in seeking the best location for Yvonne's interview when time was running out.

I thank David Noonan for information on nuclear conditions.

I acknowledge Mima Smart's, Martha Edwards' and the late Mabel Queama's statements made in *Maralinga: The Anangu Story*.

For help with the map I thank Janette Lange at the Lutheran Archives, Tom Gara, Pastor Dean Heyne, Murray Collins, Rod Shearing and Geoff Lemmy at the Royal Geographic Society of South Australia, and the Map Section at the State Library of South Australia.

For help with botanical certification I thank Bill Dowling, Secretary of the Friends of the Great Victoria Desert, and for language information I thank Paul Eckert of the Bible Society of Australia, Tom Gara, Bob Sim of Yalata Anangu School, and Rosie Bilney and others at Tullawon Health Service.

Sources

INTERVIEWS AND STATEMENTS
Yvonne Edwards was interviewed in 2006 for *Maralinga: The Anangu Story* and had conversations with the author from 2006 to 2012. Information has also been taken from Yvonne's interview for ABC's *Message Stick* (2009).

Other informants are listed in the Acknowledgements.

BOOKS, REPORTS AND PRINTED MATTER
Cane, Scott. *Pila Nguru: The Spinifex People*. Fremantle, Fremantle Arts Centre Press, 2002.

Eames, G. M. and A. C. Collett. *Final submission by Counsel on behalf of Aboriginal organisations and individuals to the Royal Commission into British Nuclear Tests in Australia*, 1985.

Edwards, Yvonne with Brenda Day and Tjitji Tjuta: *Going for Kalta: hunting for sleepy lizards at Yalata*. Alice Springs, Jukurrpa Books, IAD Press, 1997.

Mattingley, Christobel and Ken Hampton. *Survival in Our Own Land: 'Aboriginal' experiences in 'South Australia' since 1836*. Adelaide, Wakefield Press, 1988 (including Chapter 10. Edwards, W. H. 'Aboriginal land rights').

Miller, Eileen, ed. *In Loving Memory* funeral booklets, Yalata, Yvonne Edwards, 2012, David Edwards, 2004, Jamie Edwards, 2011.

Parkinson, Alan. *Maralinga: Australia's Nuclear Waste Cover-up*. Sydney, ABC Books, 2007.

Maralinga Rehabilitation Technical Advisory Committee. *Rehabilitation of former nuclear test sites at Emu and Maralinga (Australia)*. Canberra, Department of Education, Science and Training, 2002.

Yalata and Oak Valley Communities with Christobel Mattingley. *Maralinga: The Anangu Story*. Allen & Unwin, 2009.

FURTHER READING
Keane, John. 'Maralinga's Afterlife.' *The Age*, 11 May, 2003.

Timeline

1788	First Fleet lands in Botany Bay, establishing the first European settlement in Australia.
1836	State of South Australia and the city of Adelaide are founded.
1840	Beginning of the incursion into Anangu Lands by *walypala* explorer Edward John Eyre.
1870	Well-sinkers Venning and Howie come to Ooldea Soak.
1875	Ernest Giles names Anangu lands the 'Great Victoria Desert' and uses Ooldea Soak as a base camp. William Tietkens sinks and timbers a well at Ooldea and records 'native dams' elsewhere.
1880s	First pastoralist arrives with sheep and sinks another well. Kangaroo shooters arrive and set up camp at the Soak.
1890s	Elder Expedition explores Anangu lands. Richard Maurice records five 'native dams'.
1901	Government surveyor J.G. Stewart passes through Ooldea searching for route for proposed East–West railway.
1904	Government prospector Frank George records ten 'native wells'.
1912	Work begins on construction of the Transcontinental Railway, and construction workers introduce tobacco, tea, sugar, white flour, guns and alcohol into Anangu society, trading them for women.
1913	First children of *walypala* fathers born.
1917	17 OCTOBER: construction of Transcontinental Railway completed. Depletion of water in Ooldea Soak continues with Commonwealth Railways 'acquiring' the Soak, sinking a bore and pumping over 45 000 litres daily for steam locomotives and staff at sidings. Desert oaks which stabilised the dunes and provided shelter for

	Anangu cut down for firewood for a condensing plant. Cast-off garments sent from Adelaide to make Anangu 'decent' for the benefit of train travellers. Commonwealth Railways regulation decrees: 'No native, however clean or well-dressed, may travel on the East–West line, unless special permission is given.'
1918	Ornithologist S. A. White reports: 'The country round (Ooldea) has been trampled almost out of recognition (by camel teams).' Daisy Bates sets up camp between the Soak and Ooldea Siding, trying to keep Anangu from destructive influences.
1920	Daisy Bates arranges Anangu display at Cook for Prince of Wales, who visits for two and a half hours.
1923	Ooldea Soak water becomes brackish from over-extraction. Only one well from the 50 dug still functional. Beginning of severe drought across the region, causing more Anangu to move to the Soak.
1933	Annie Lock of the United Aborigines Mission (UAM) arrives at Ooldea and sets up camp.
1934	Annie Lock arranges Anangu display for the Duke of Gloucester.
1935	Daisy Bates leaves Ooldea to live near Adelaide.
1936	Harrie Green and his wife Marion arrive to establish the UAM Mission at the Soak.
1938	SA Government proclaims an Aboriginal Reserve of 2000 square miles including the Soak. Gradually UAM establishes a ration depot giving out tea, sugar, flour and clothing, along with a school, a church, dormitories for 60 children, and a bathroom and a dining room. Father Christmas arrives at Ooldea.
1942	2 AUGUST: David Edwards born at Ooldea.
1943–4	Aboriginal groups still coming in to the Soak from the Spinifex country in the north-west because of drought.
1944	Sixteen young Anangu baptised at a well at Ooldea.
Late 1940s	
	Single Anangu men sent to work on distant sheep and cattle stations and young couples sent off their own country to UAM Mission at Gerard on the River Murray, SA.

1946	Australian Government agrees to allow British Government to test long-range weapons on Anangu country.
1947	Long Range Weapons Establishment builds a base at Woomera and begins rocket testing trials. Native Patrol Officer Walter MacDougall appointed by Long Range Weapons Establishment to patrol over 100 000 square kilometres without a vehicle to contact Anangu groups.
1950	12 SEPTEMBER: Tjintjiwara born in the bush at Ooldea and named Yvonne by the missionaries.
1951	SA Government acquires a station property near Fowlers Bay. Whitefella farmers object to Anangu occupation, so they are given the productive eastern area, and the western remainder of the property, Yalata, is retained for future solution to Ooldea's problems.
1952	24 JUNE: Ooldea Mission closes without prior notice because of row between UAM federal council and the SA branch. Anangu expelled and dispersed east, north and west. SA Government asks the Lutheran Mission at Koonibba to the east to resettle the people at Yalata.
1952	David Edwards placed in the Koonibba Mission Children's Home. Yvonne and family moved to Ooldea Tank at Monburu on Yalata lands, not their traditional country.
1953	Permission given to the British Government by Australian Government to test atomic weapons on traditional Anangu lands.
1953	15 OCTOBER: first British atomic test series, Operation Totem, explodes two bombs, the first of 10 kilotons at Emu Field, contravening safe firing weather conditions, causing death, blindness and chronic illness to Anangu at Wallatinna and surrounding areas.
1953–63	Yvonne is growing up while so-called Minor Trials at Maralinga release almost 100 kilograms of radioactive and toxic elements including uranium and plutonium.
1954	The Aboriginal Reserve that included Ooldea Soak is revoked at request of Prime Minister Menzies.

1955	Great Victoria Desert declared a Prohibited Area. Anangu officially banned from their own traditional lands.
C. 1955–7	Yvonne and family living in Big Camp. Yvonne attends walkabout school.
1956	18 MAY: Yvonne baptised at Monburu.
1956	27 SEPTEMBER: Operation Buffalo commences at Maralinga with detonation of a 15 kiloton bomb. Three more bombs detonated over the next 25 days. Yvonne is six years old.
1957	9 OCTOBER: Operation Antler, with three explosions, culminating in biggest bomb of 25 kilotons. Yvonne is seven years old. Altogether almost 100 kilotons (100 000 tonnes) of explosive dropped between 1953–7 in the three series of tests.
C. 1958–9	Yvonne lives with foster families at Fowlers Bay to attend school.
1961	Six containers of plutonium fragments placed in concrete pits at Maralinga Airfield Cemetery. They remain there until 1978 when they are repatriated to the UK.
1963	5 MAY: Yvonne confirmed in the Lutheran Church of the Good Shepherd at Yalata.
1964	Operation Hercules V temporary clean-up ploughs and grades plutonium contamination into the soil as a temporary measure but plutonium hazard is estimated to last for 24 000 years.
1964	Yalata has population of 350, water shortage and unemployment problems.
1965	Drinking rights for Aboriginal people introduced.
1965	10 AUGUST: Yvonne and David's first child, Michael, born; removed by Welfare for adoption soon after.
1966	Operation Brumby. British Government's second and final clean-up creates more problems by concentrating contamination and creating hot spots, and making insufficient records.
1967	24 JULY: Yvonne and David marry at Koonibba.

1974	Salvage rights at Maralinga Village granted to the Yalata Community. David Edwards and some other Anangu men employed but not issued with protective clothing. Families accompany them and live in the village.
1975	Lutheran Church hands over management of Yalata community to the newly incorporated Yalata Community Council.
Late 1970s	
	Yalata Roadhouse established to sell artefacts and paintings.
1981	Yalata Community Council begins discussions with SA Government for return of their lands.
1984	*Maralinga Tjarutja Land Rights Act* finally passed. Official documents handed over in the bush near Maralinga on 18 December.
1984–5	Royal Commission into British Nuclear Tests in Australia.
1985	Yvonne and David find Michael and are welcomed by his adoptive family.
1991	Delegation of Anangu elders flies to London to lobby the British Government for compensation.
1992	Delegation returns to London to pursue claim.
1995	British Government finally contributes money for clean-up and compensation.
1995	Yvonne and three others write to the Liquor Commissioner asking for tighter restrictions on alcohol outlets.
1997	Yvonne appointed to the Wangka Wilurrara Regional Council. Yvonne works on the book *Going for Kalta*.
1999	*Going for Kalta* wins the Children's Book Council of Australia Eve Pownall Award for Information Books.
1998	Two more sections of land handed back after remedial work.
1999	Yvonne commissioned to make a *kuturu* for the Sisters of St Joseph.
2003	David diagnosed with cancer. Yvonne moves to Adelaide to be with him as he undergoes treatment.

2004	21 SEPTEMBER: David dies.
2006	Yalata Roadhouse closed because of asbestos.
2006–7	Yvonne and others work on creating *Maralinga: The A̱nangu Story*.
2008	Michael dies after a road accident. Yvonne's grandson Dominic born with stomach defect.
2009	Patrick diagnosed with cancer. *Maralinga: The A̱nangu Story* launched at Tandanya Aboriginal Cultural Institute before a crowd of over 400. Yvonne and others interviewed by ABC. ABC's *Message Stick* makes two documentaries based on the book.
2009	18 DECEMBER: Section 400 handed back at Maralinga Village.
2010	Patrick dies. Yvonne turns 60. Paintings for *Maralinga: The A̱nangu Story* displayed at the International Women's Day Exhibition. Gladys Elphick Award to 'The Twelve Strong A̱nangu Women' given to the informants and artists for *Maralinga: The A̱nangu Story* which was an Honour Book in the Children's Book Council of Australia 2010 awards.
2011	Jamie dies of cancer.
2012	7 MARCH: Yvonne phones to say she is ready to start work on her book. 15 MARCH: She collapses and is rushed to hospital. 7 APRIL: Yvonne dies. Yvonne's funeral at Yalata on 27 April.
2014	5 NOVEMBER: Final section of Maralinga lands handed back to traditional owners.

Aboriginal people traditionally measure time by the sun, stars and seasons.

Index

Page references: in **bold** refer to images/in *italics* refer to endmatter

Aboriginal and Torres Strait Islander Commission (ATSIC) 74
Airport, Maralinga International 60
alcohol 71, 76, 80–1, 91, 97, 142, *189*, *193*
Anangu law (*Tjukurpa*) 5
art 14, 74, 83–4, **85**, 88–93, 124–5, 141–2, 149–54, 175, *193*
artefacts **4**, 17, **72–3**, 76, 83–4, **85**, 97, 149, *193*
artwork by Edwards, Yvonne
  Bush tucker **92**
  Coming home to family **114**, **119**
  Crucifixion 154, **155**, **162**
  Gathering **vi**, **122**
  Kangaroo, red (*malu*) entrails **68**
  kuturu stick 84, **84–5**
  Malu (red kangaroo) and *kalaya* (emu), 2009 **26**
  Maralinga [I] **22**, **128**, **142**, **143**, **146**, **180**
  Maralinga [II] **38**, **54**, **94–5**
  Munda (country) with spinifex (centre) surrounded by different ochres **172**
  Nativity **89**
  Seven Sisters **89**, **140**, 153
  Teaching inma (*dance*), 2008 **16**
  Teaching our culture, 2007 **46**, **96**
  Wanampi and waterholes **82**, **90**
  Wanampi at waterhole **28**, **50**
  Wanampi family at waterhole **8**, **20**
  Wanampi, the Rainbow Serpent **x**, **25**
Aspinall, Anita and Don 115–18, 144–5
Aspinall, Michael 51–3, 115–25, 144–5, 147, 166, 177
Aspinall, Richard 125
atomic bomb/nuclear testing 23, 39–44, **41**, 93, **94–5**, 127, 129, 131, 142, 154, 156–61, 166, 174–5, 177–8, 181
  Totem Series, 1953 40, *191*
  Minor Trials, 1953–63 41, 62, 181
  Buffalo Series, 1956 40
  Antler Series, 1957 43
Baker, Jack **77**
basket-making **112**
Bates, Daisy 7, *190*
birthing, Anangu 9
Brown, Mavis Tymunee 29, **30**
Bryant, Rita 83
bush medicine 10, 76, 99, 166, 176
bush tucker **6**, 60–1, 76, 91, **92**, 99, 102, 107, 124, 142, *Bush tucker* **92**
cancer 67, 107, 110, 131–2, 134–5, 137–9, 150, 161, 164, 177–8
caring for country 1, 44, 70–1
carving 17, **72**, 83–4, 166
Ceduna 76, 84, 113, **182–3**
  Ceduna Aboriginal Arts and Cultural Centre 88
Christianity 7, 18, 120, 144, 163, 161–7
Clark, Pastor Bryce 110, 113
Clark, Judy 113
clean-up and salvaging, Maralinga 57, 131–2, *192–3 see also* radioactive poisoning
clothes 7, 33
Collecting Maku/story 74
Coming home to family **114**, **119**
connection with country 44, 70–1, 88
Cox, Alice 67, 127, 151, 158
Cox, Leanne **112**
Craig, David and Ruth 49–50
Cresp, Sister Mary 84
Crucifixion 154, **155**, **162**
Day, Brenda 99, *188*
Diment, Pam 88
Dobbins, Eve 73–4
Dreamtime Ancestors 5, 17, 70

195

drugs 76, 80–1
Dunn, Helen 113
Edwards, Aaron 55, **66**, 80–1,
  108, **109**, 147–8, **157**, 161,
  164, 178
Edwards, David 47, **49**, 51,
  55–7, **66**, **72**, 72–9, 83–4,
  115, 118, 120–7, 131–7,
  147–8, 156, 158, 161, 166,
  177, *190–4*
Edwards, Dominic 147–8,
  156, 178, *194*
Edwards, Duane 55, 57,
  62, 108
Edwards, Jamie 55, 161, 166,
  178, *188*, *194*
Edwards, Judy 55, **66**, 98,
  108, **111**, 137
Edwards, Kristy 147–8, 164
Edwards, Martha 29, 62, 70
Edwards, Patrick 55, 150,
  161, 166, 178, 179, *194*
Edwards, Taylor
  Noreen 164–5
Edwards, Teddy 55, 57, 62,
  67, 108
Edwards, Terence 55, **66**,
  108, **109**
Edwards, Yvonne, artwork by
  Bush tucker **92**
  Coming home to family **114**,
  119
  Crucifixion 154, **155**, **162**
  Gathering **vi**, **122**
  Kangaroo, red (malu)
  entrails **68**
  kuturu stick 84, **84–5**
  *Malu (red kangaroo) and
  kalaya (emu)*, 2009 **26**
  Maralinga [I] **22**, **128**, **142**,
  143, **146**, **180**
  Maralinga [III] **38**, **54**, **94–5**
  *Munda (country) with
  spinifex (centre) surrounded
  by different ochres* **172**

Nativity **89**
Seven Sisters **89**, **140**, 153
Teaching inma *(dance)*,
  2008 **16**
Teaching our culture,
  2007 **46**, **96**
Wanampi *and waterholes*
  82, **90**
Wanampi *at waterhole* **28**,
  50
Wanampi *family at
  waterhole* **8**, **20**
Wanampi, *the Rainbow
  Serpent* **x**, **25**
emu (*kalaya*) **6**, **26**, 61, 160
English language 18, 34
Fiedler, Grant 74
food gathering and
  hunting 60–1, 76, **92**, 97,
  99, 102–4, 108, 131
Fowlers Bay 34–6, **182–3**
Gathering **vi**, **122**
Gibson, Harry **45**
Giles, Bob 29
*Going for Kalta: hunting for
  sleepy lizards at Yalata* 99,
  100-1, 102
grief 21, 27, 51, 53, 67, 70–1,
  129, 132, 139, 156, 161,
  167, 177
gudia (Western myall) 83,
  86–7, 166
Heyne, Pastor Deane 75, 110
hunting and food
  gathering 60–1, 76, **92**, 97,
  99, 102–4, 108, 131
illness and death from
  radiation 40, 64–5, 67, 79,
  93, **94–5**, 129, 139, 142,
  150–3, 156, 158, 161, 164,
  177–8
inma (song, dance,
  celebration) 4, 24
kalaya (emu) **6**, **26**, 61, 160
kalta (lizard) **6**, 24, **92**, 99,

100-1, 102–3, 166
kangaroo, red (*malu*) 5, **6**, **26**,
  27, 51, 60–1, 160
Kangaroo, red (malu)
  entrails **68**
Kelly, Matthew 110
kinship system 52
Koonibba 21, 47, 55, **182–3**
Kugena, Maureen 74
kuturu (stick) **16**, 84, **84–5**
language, Pitjantjatjara 17,
  34, 52, 74, 118, 124
laundry 7, 9, 31, **32**
Lester, Yami 40, 151
lizard (*kalta*) **6**, 24, **92**, 99,
  100-1, 102–3, 166
Lutheran mission 21, 31, 36,
  45, 47, 55
  Children's Home 47
MacArthur, Josie 98, **112**,
  138, **151**, 176
MacDougall, Walter 44
Madigan, Michele 99
maku (witchetty grubs) 2, **6**,
  60, **92**, 160, 165
malu (red kangaroo) 5, **6**, **26**,
  27, 51, 60–1, 160
*Malu (red kangaroo) and
  kalaya (emu)*, 2009 **26**
malukuru (Sturt's desert
  pea) 14, **15**, 149, 158, **170-1**
Maralinga [I] **22**, **128**, **142**,
  143, **146**, **180**
Maralinga [III] **38**, **54**, **94–5**
Maralinga, big hall 57–8
*Maralinga: The Anangu
  Story* 103, 141, **142–3**, 144,
  150–4, 158, 161, 165, 174–6
Maralinga Tjarutja 77–8,
  154, **157**, **159**, 181, **182–3**
*Maralinga Tjarutja Land
  Rights Act*, 1984, the 76–8
marriage 55
May, Margaret 62, 67
Miller, Eileen 98, *188*

Milpuddie, Edie 127
missionaries 7, 71
Monburu (*also see* Ooldea Tank) 31, 103, 133, **182–3**, *191*, *193*
Munda *(country) with spinifex (centre) surrounded by different ochres* 172
Murka, Colin 29, **45**, 62, 144, 176
Murka, Noreen 29, 164
Murka, Ronald 29, **45**
Murka, Tommy 29, **30**
Nativity 89
Ngura Wiya (No-Go Zone) 160
No-Go Zone (*Ngura Wiya*) 160
Nundroo 76, 80–1, **182–3**
Oak Valley **12–13**, 65, 67, 78, 144, 151, **182–3**
Ooldea 5, 7, 9, 17–20, 47, 67, 70–1, **182–3**
Ooldea mallee 10, **11**
Ooldea Soak (*Yuldi*) 4, 5
Ooldea Tank 29, 33, **182–3**
Operation Brumby 57
Penong 76, 80–1, **182–3**
petrol sniffing 80–1, 97
Pitjantjatjara language 17, 34, 52, 74, 118, 124
prohibited area **61**
Queama, Mabel, the late 65, 127
Queama, Tommy **77**
radioactive poisoning 27, 40–3, 57–8, 61, 64–5, 67, 78–9, 93, 129, 131–2, 139, 148, 158, 160, 181
rations, government 7, 31–3, **32**, 71
relocation from Ooldea 18, 20–21, 69–71, 129, 155, 169
return of lands 76–8, 154–60, **157**, **159**, *193*

Royal Commission into British Nuclear Tests in South Australia, 1984 127, 132, 174, *193*
Royal Flying Doctor Service 73
Sandimar, Brenton **111**
Sandimar, Kaylene **157**
Sandimar, Marjorie 74, **157**
Sandimar, Rene 17–18, 43, 84, 127
Sandimar, Thomas **157**
school 33–5, **34**
seasons 2, 7, 14, 78, 158, *194*
Seven Sisters **89**, **140**, 153
Sim, Bob 91
Sisters of St Joseph 84, *193*
Smart, Mima 62, 64, 70, 79, 113, 144, **151**, 174, 176
song, dance (*inma*), celebration 4, 24
sorry business 98, 129–31, 137, 166–7
Stewart, Maria **45**
Stolen Generation 51, 115–21, 123
Sturt's desert pea (*ma<u>l</u>uku<u>r</u>u*) 14, **15**, 149, 158, **170-1**
Surch, Val 104–8, **112**
Tandanya National Aboriginal Cultural Institute, Adelaide 151, *194*
Taranaki **42**, 65
Teaching inma *(dance)*, 2008 **16**
Teaching our culture, 2007 **46**, **96**
time (*also see* seasons) 14, 158, *194*
Tjinnalumba Tank 31, **32**, 133, **182–3**
Tracks by Michael Aspinall 126
Transcontinental Railway 5

Tschuna, Desmond 98
Tullawon Health Service 72–3, 91
United Aborigines Mission (UAM) 9, 18, 47, *190–1*
walkabout 31, 33, *192*
walkabout school 33–5
Wa<u>n</u>ampi *and waterholes* **82**, **90**
Wa<u>n</u>ampi *at waterhole* **28**, **50**
Wa<u>n</u>ampi *family at waterhole* **8**, **20**
Wa<u>n</u>ampi, *the Rainbow Serpent* **x**, **25**
Wa<u>n</u>ampi, the Rainbow Serpent, provider of water **x**, **1**, **8**, **20**, 24, **25**, **28**, 31, **50**, 70, **82**, 87, **90**, 91, 142
Wangka Wilurrara Women's Advisory Committee 74
Watson 60, 62
watu (wombat) 103–4, 165
Welfare, the 51, 123
West, Joy **109**
white arrival 5
witchetty grub (*maku*) 2, **6**, 60, **92**, 160, 165
wombat (*watu*) 103–4, 165
Women's Centre, the 83, 104
work 55–6, 65, 72, 74
Yalata **34**, 36, 39, 43, 47, 58, 70–3, 78, **79**, 80, 145, **182–3**
Yalata A<u>n</u>angu School 49–50, 74, 91
Yalata Cemetery 93, **94–5**, 129, **130**, **136**, 167
Yalata Community Council 57, 72–3, 125
Yalata football team 75
Yalata netball team 75, **75**
Yalata Roadhouse 84
Yalata Women's Choir 75
Yalata/story 74

ALSO AVAILABLE FROM ALLEN & UNWIN

'*Maralinga – The Anangu Story* is our story. We have told it for our children, our grandchildren and their children. We have told it for you.'

In words and pictures Yalata and Oak Valley community members, with author Christobel Mattingley, describe what happened in the Maralinga Tjarutja lands of South Australia before the bombs and after.